John Lancaster Spalding

**Things of the mind**

John Lancaster Spalding

**Things of the mind**

ISBN/EAN: 9783742862860

Manufactured in Europe, USA, Canada, Australia, Japa

Cover: Foto ©ninafisch / pixelio.de

Manufactured and distributed by brebook publishing software (www.brebook.com)

John Lancaster Spalding

**Things of the mind**

# THINGS OF THE MIND

### By Bishop Spalding.

THOUGHTS AND THEORIES OF LIFE AND EDUCATION. 16mo. $1.00.
EDUCATION AND THE HIGHER LIFE. 12mo. $1.00.
THINGS OF THE MIND. 12mo. $1.00.
MEANS AND ENDS OF EDUCATION. 12mo. $1.00.
SONGS: CHIEFLY FROM THE GERMAN. 16mo, gilt top. $1.25.

A. C. McCLURG AND CO.
CHICAGO.

# THINGS OF THE MIND

BY

## J. L. SPALDING
### Bishop of Peoria

A genuine interest in problems of education helps to keep us young, for it carries us back to our own springtime and to the company of children. It is also an evidence that we ourselves have not ceased to grow, and are therefore not yet old.

CHICAGO
A. C. McCLURG AND COMPANY
1899

COPYRIGHT
BY A. C. MCCLURG & CO.
A. D. 1894

# CONTENTS.

| Chapter | | Page |
|---|---|---|
| I. | Views of Education | 7 |
| II. | Views of Education | 40 |
| III. | Views of Education | 66 |
| IV. | Professional Education | 94 |
| V. | Theories of Life and Education | 128 |
| VI. | Culture and Religion | 173 |
| VII. | Patriotism | 220 |

# THINGS OF THE MIND.

## CHAPTER I.

### VIEWS OF EDUCATION.

*To be an interpreter and relater of the best and sagest things among mine own citizens.* — MILTON.

WHETHER it be beautiful scenery, or noble monuments, or venerable ruins, or painting, or sculpture, or music, or books, or contact with life, things presented to us educate us only inasmuch as we react upon them. Lead the listless savage through all that is most worth seeing, knowing, admiring, and loving, and at the end he is what he was at the start. The general problem of education is how best to place instinct and passion under the control of reason and conscience, of higher motives and tastes, that men may learn to find their pleasure and their happiness in doing what brings health, knowledge, and virtue. The educator's aim is to create interest, for thus alone is it possible to awaken mind. How often it happens, where dulness and listlessness had prevailed, a new-comer brings joy and fresh thoughts. This the teacher should do; when he appears, he should call forth a sense of glad expectancy, just as a true actor at once lifts a heavy scene into the region of active interest. He is wholly free from the pedant's vanity and conceit, and in his skill there is the play of life. Mechanical iteration is the radical fault in education. We pardon our instructors almost anything if only they be not tiresome. Better not to teach or preach than to weary. When the pupil's intercourse with the teacher opens to him glimpses into higher worlds, he is quick to believe all that is told him of heroes, saints, and sages. Sowers, reapers, and gardeners, hunters, fishermen, and the feeders of flocks are the best society for boys; they stimulate an observant interest in the things which are always around them, and touch the sources of pure delight in nature in her most beneficent and pleasant manifestations. To watch, when one is young, the sun with gradual wheel sink slowly from sight, or the stars, as one by one they break upon the view, or the birds when with gentle flutterings they settle to rest amid the leaves, or the full-fed cattle as they lie in wakeful dreams, or the young of animals disporting themselves upon the green, or the bees plying their task amid the flowers, or ants providing their hoard, or any of the thousand things nature offers so prodigally to our gaze, — is to drink at the purest and freshest fountain of knowledge, is to store the mind with thoughts and images which, as the years go on, remain with us fragrant and wholesome as a breath of air from life's fair dawn. To look on the fierce battles of bulls, of boars, and of cocks is to feel the might of courage and endurance. To see the little martens as they sally forth to attack the hawk is to learn what pluck and daring, what a union of several may accomplish. The great source of sympathy with mankind, as with nature, are those early recollections which bring back to us fathers and mothers, brothers and sisters, and all the fair, fresh world which circled about our childhood. Read no book unless it interest thee. When thou readest, or speakest, or hearest, look steadfastly with the mind at the things the words symbolize. If there be question of mountains, let them loom before thee; if of the ocean, let its billows roll beneath thy eyes. This habit will give to thy voice even pliancy and meaning. The more sources of interest we have, the richer is our life. To hold any portion of truth in a vital way is better than to have its whole baggage stored merely in one's memory. The self-taught look at the world with their own eyes and think their own thoughts. Thy own mind is the first and final court of evidence, and what it receives it should receive on the authority of evidence or on the evidence of authority; in other words, it should accept only what it sees to be true, or has sufficient warrant for believing. The more cultivated a man is, the greater the number of things which interest him. Where others see nothing he finds a well-spring of fresh thoughts; he observes, and attends to what he observes; he receives much because he brings much; he discovers truth and beauty and goodness in things because he bears them within himself. His mind is a light which clothes what he contemplates in well-defined forms and rightly shaded colors; his heart is an alembic in which the fine spirit of love is distilled; his imagination, like a god, calls forth a living world from the waste and void abyss of matter. He who thinks for himself is rarely persuaded by another. Information and inspiration he gladly receives, but he forms his own judgment. Arguments and reasons which to the thoughtful sound like mockery satisfy the superficial and the ignorant. An enlightened mind sympathizes with the multitude as he sympathizes with children, not so much for what they are as for what it is possible to make of them.

"To be a fool after the fashion," says Kant, "is better than to be a downright fool." Noble thoughts and pure loves inform the countenance, and give dignity and grace to one's whole bearing. A fair and luminous soul makes its body beautiful. Take up anew each day the task set thee, — to make thyself more truly a rational, social, and moral being.

**Hasteless, but restless, O my soul, follow after the light
That still gleams as brightly as the stars that follow the night.**

Man is not born, he is made by education, — by the education he receives and by the education he gives himself. Imagination rules our life. It creates the ideals by which we live; from point to point it beckons us on to the unattained. Over vulgar reality it throws a mystic veil; it draws the charmed circle wherein move friendship, love, and freedom. It blows the trumpet of honor and fame; it leads the way to glorious death.

Superficial minds are fond of dwelling upon the evils religion has wrought; but serious thinkers know that the ever open and inexhaustible fountain of faith, hope, and love, is belief in God, — or in gods, if you will.

If men have fought and persecuted and died for their religion, it is because they have held it to be a priceless blessing. This breath from higher worlds, unseen but felt to be real, is to young unfolding souls what sunshine and rain are to the growing corn.

When the vital current flows rich and healthful, as in the young, life is believed, without the remotest shadow of doubt, to be good; but this is largely unconscious life, and the question is, whether consciousness is a blessing, whether to see things as they are brings joy and peace. The problem therefore resolves itself into this, — whether, at the heart of being, behind, within, and above all, there is truth and love; in other words, whether the ultimate fact is conscious life. They who are unable to think that this is so must hold that to think is to be sad, whereas they who believe in God cannot but think that the misery of conscious existence is accidental. Theism is optimism, atheism is pessimism. If there were no God, ignorance would be bliss, and education a crime. Hope and love are the expression of faith in life's goodness. He alone is a true pessimist who neither hopes nor loves. The end of education is the formation of character; character rests on the basis of morality; and morality, if it have life and vigor, is interfused with religion. True religion is inseparable from morality, and morality from right life, and therefore from right education. Hence religion, morality, and education, are a trinity. "Religion," says Herbart, "will never hold the tranquil place in the depths of the heart which it ought to have, if its fundamental ideas are not among the earliest which belong to recollection, — if it is not bound up and blended with all that changing life leaves behind in the centre of personality." As we should strive to teach ourselves to take delight in whatever is fair in nature, in whatever is true or beautiful in literature or art, so we should learn to find pleasure in whatever brings good to men, and first of all in the welfare and success of those around us, though they be our foes and rivals. A noble man feels that no human being, not even his enemy, is as happy as he would have him be, and thus he finds satisfaction in what only embitters and saddens mean and narrow souls. This enlightened good-will which enables us to have genuine sympathy with all men, is the very soul of the moral character which it is the aim and end of education to form. Why do men choose an avocation? To gain a livelihood. But the better sort, whatever their special occupation, labor to fit themselves for life in the higher world of thought and love. Let every faculty be developed in the mild and wholesome air of religion. Good teachers feel they are educating themselves as well as their pupils, and when this belief is not found the power to educate is lacking. He who is led by the ideal of intellectual culture concerns himself little with mere questions of social order and political economy, for he feels that if he can but make reason prevail it will put right whatever may need ordering. They who are able to draw forth the mind and illumine the soul should be relieved from all other tasks. In our social gatherings we ascend from out the true self, to glide on the surface amid the forms and shows of life. Hence nothing deeply interesting is ever heard where men meet to eat and talk. Do what it is right thou shouldst do now; but strive ceaselessly that it may become possible for thee to do the work thou wast born to do.

The craving for applause is as morbid as the craving for alcohol. He alone is strong who is self-sufficient, since he is what he is through communion with God and the world of truth. When the great man — poet, philosopher, statesman, orator, or captain — has gained recognition, he becomes indifferent to the praise he once longed for. Happier is he who dies knowing his own worth, himself unknown, "and what most merits fame in silence hid." Let the young be made to understand that the desire to appear, to be seen, to be noticed, to be talked of, springs from a crude and barbarous nature. When we look to changes to be wrought in the social and religious world, it may be permitted to feel discouragement, but when there is question of upbuilding and transforming our own being we should be filled with a divine confidence, knowing that the aids to noble life, like the kingdom of God, lie within us. Be a man, not a partisan. "Great moral energy," says Herbart, "is the result of broad views and of whole unbroken masses of thought." Every secret, for those who can see, is an open secret. How any man achieved any godlike thing, any man may know.

Thou mayst not be an artist who works in stone or on canvas, or who breathes harmonious numbers, but an artist thou shouldst become, in the ceaseless effort to fashion thy own life into the likeness of what is true, beautiful, and good. Though thou shouldst think all the world a stage, learn at least, like Augustus, to play well thy part. For a century now and more, the world resounds with much speech about the rights of man. His first and chief right is the right to grow, to unfold his being on many sides, and to bring himself into conscious harmony with all that is. Heed not the tempter's voice, seeking to persuade thee thou hast done thy best. To have done the best he can is little for the man who feels that his ever urgent duty is to make himself capable of still better things by pushing day by day into wider and serener worlds. Each man is the maker of himself, the power he uses being God's; and each present moment bears within itself the future's form and substance. To be a man is to be a fighter, a combatant on the world's wide battlefield, where the cohorts of ignorance and sin wage ceaseless warfare against the soul. No one is by nature good or great or wise, but whoever attains such height reaches it by hard toil and long struggles with temptations and hindrances of many kinds. Education lays the foundation, self-education erects the building. Another may show the way, but if we would reach the goal we must ourselves walk therein. Whatever may strengthen body, mind, or soul, the educator needs and should make use of. The strong man, in the right sense, is also wise and good, helpful and loving. They who starve the body cannot nourish the mind, and if the heads of institutions of learning have not the means to supply copious, wholesome food, they should be made to withdraw from the business of education; but if, having the means, they seek to save money at the expense of health and life, they should be dealt with as criminals. To educate to passive obedience is to predestine to failure.

When Demosthenes was asked what makes an orator, he replied, "Action, action, action." Had the question been, "What makes a man?" the answer should have been the same, — "Action, action, action." We know what will is only when we begin to act, for action begets will. When we clearly see a thing to be possible we have begun to teach ourselves how to make it real. The circle of thought which we create for ourselves and in which we habitually move, makes us what we are. As the gardener by engrafting can produce the most precious fruit from an inferior stock, so the educator, by implanting fresh thoughts and principles, new aims and desires in the mind of his pupil, may recreate and transform his whole being. The supreme problem for the individual, the family, the school, the State, and the Church, is how to harmonize liberty with order. The higher the source of authority, and the head of rule, the easier the solution. The rhythmic movement of life is the mark of health in the physical, the domestic, and the social body. In every ill-ordered household there is degeneracy.

The power within and behind nature is the power within and behind man, and the more we realize that we are part of nature, that what we call nature is a force which streams through us as a type of law and order, of wisdom and harmony, of strength and goodness, the more do we advance in dignity of being as rational and moral men. Endowments are possibilities merely; each one's self-activity must determine what for him they shall become.

When we say man is born free we mean nothing more than that he is born capable of making himself free by a process of gradual emancipation from the thraldom of ignorance, selfishness, and sensuality. This, self-education must accomplish for him. In a world where multitudes strive for knowledge, power, and wealth, the indolent and the listless are made use of or thrust back. The law of affinity, beginning with chemical atoms, runs upward to souls and God. The mind is drawn to what is akin to it, as planets are drawn to suns.

Our talents come to us largely from our social

inheritance and environment, and they should be used for the common good. We begin with studying how to learn, and we end with learning how to study. The more we advance the more conscious we become of obeying ideal aims and ends. Only he who strives to distinguish himself, to make himself different from the crowd around him, becomes wise and strong. Be many kinds of man, but be sincere and high. What a wise man knows and loves is more interesting than himself, and if he write he will write of that, not of himself. The proper attitude of the mind toward the objective world is that of philosophical indifference. Things are what they are, and we, too, from moment to moment, are what we are; let the relation be seen and recognized. Beware of the will-o'-the-wisp which would lead thee to defend whatever thou mayst at any time have said or written. Little of what the best have written has significance for more than one generation. They who have learned most have had most to unlearn.

All the child and youth has been taught, the man must relearn if he is to arrive at insight. Possession makes us indifferent or self-satisfied; the ceaseless striving after better things makes us men. When we consider the diseases to which man is subject it seems marvellous that any one should have good health; and when we attend to the innumerable sources of his errors, it seems almost incredible that any one should think and judge rightly; for his mind is swayed from the line of truth by youth and by age, by ignorance and by learning, by feebleness, as by excessive vigor of body, by imagination, and by the lack of it, by love and by hate, by hope and by despair, by wealth and by poverty, by sluggishness and by haste, by fear and by envy, by lust and by greed, by pride and by conceit, by rationalism and by fanaticism, by cowardice and by hypocrisy, by credulity and by incredulity. How then shall he learn to see things as they are? Not malice and self-interest alone, but pity, sympathy, love, and prudence prompt us to deceive. The truth is sometimes cruel and brutal, or shocking in its nakedness, and they who soften its harshness, or throw a veil over its hideousness, will not believe they are wicked. The mother hides it from her child, the physician from his patient. We soon learn all our friends have to tell us; our intellectual shocks and surprises come from those who disagree with us, and they are our best teachers. The more we know, the more we doubt. Doubt is the shadow which the splendor of truth as it falls upon the mind always casts.  It is easy to speak or write of what we know little; they whose knowledge is large and profound find less to say.  Whoever turns his mind habitually and strongly in a given direction will find that, little by little, it loses the power of taking any other.  The scientist becomes unable to think poetically or religiously; the poet and the mystic lose sight of the definiteness of things.  Thus the soul, like the body, is subdued to what it works in.  No state of things is good, no theory is practice, the real is never the ideal, — the spirit whereby and wherein thou livest and workest is the all in all.

> O for a thrill of love, a thrill from life's fair prime,
> To make my being start and blossom into rhyme,
> Bring heaven near and give to stars their appealing light
> And to my soul the wings which tempt infinite flight.
> By love we live, when love is dead all things are dead,
> And in a world we move whence God and the soul have fled.

"Never," says Jean Paul, "has one forgotten his pure, right-educating mother.  On the blue mountains of our dim childhood toward which we ever turn and look, stand the mothers who marked out to us from thence our life; the most blessed age must be forgotten ere we can forget the warmest heart."

At her death Laura appeared to Petrarch, in a dream, and holding out her hand she asked:

"Do you not remember her who influenced your youth and led you out of the common road of life?"

A woman cannot hope to make a sage or a saint or a hero of the man who loves her, but she may, of the child. Contempt for women is the mark of a crude mind or of a corrupt heart. What strength is there not in the rich joyfulness of youth, bursting forth into glad song and laughter, and passing lightly away from hardship and disappointment, out again to where the glorious sunshine plays upon the rippling waters and the happy flowers. The very memory of it all comes back to us like a message from God to bid us be stout of heart and to keep growing. Those we love sanctify for us the places where they have lived; the spots even where they have but passed are sacred.

The philosophy of life is the philosophy of education, and sympathy with the race tends to resolve itself into the desire to give to all a right culture; for it is plain that in this way better than in any other we are able to be of help to our fellows. Our interest in education is the measure of our interest in the world and in humanity. He alone is a true believer in the ideal of culture who is persuaded that culture, like virtue, is its own reward, that nothing an enlightened mind may enable him to obtain is as good as the enlightened mind itself. The aim of culture, as it is also the aim of religion, is to create an inner strength and enlightenment which supersedes and makes superfluous mere legalism.

Power of concentration, of persevering application of the whole mind to what ought to be known and done, is a mark of genius, and it is also one of the best results of right education. The educational value of the study of physical science is found in the sense it awakens of the universal presence of law and order, and also in the training to close and accurate observation which it enforces.

It is easy to educate too much, to put one's own mind and will in the place of the learner's; but we are always safe when we help the pupil to educate himself. "The mind," says Schiller, "possesses only what it does." All of us, the most ignorant even, know more than we know how to put to right use. Prejudices are idols to which we sometimes sacrifice the most precious things, — the light of the mind, the joy of the soul, the free play of the imagination, the love of truth itself, and yet a man without prejudices is like a man without a home or a country. He is a stranger who finds no fellows, no company in which he will gain recognition, for nothing makes the crowd so uncomfortable as dispassionate reason, the pure light of the intellect. It is easy to meet with well-informed minds, but we seldom find one who has a real world-view and a circle of thought in which he is at home, whose life rests upon unity of purpose, whose conduct is controlled by principle, whose thinking has truth for its single aim. In former times to assert truth was to risk life, or, at the least, loss of name and goods; but now, when there is no danger and the whole rabble rush in each with his torch to enlighten the world, truth, grown ashamed of its nakedness, hides from the eyes of men.

"Work and enthusiasm," says Goethe, "are the pinions on which great deeds are borne." If the pupil see that his teacher is mean or arbitrary, the school becomes for him a place of perversion. Language is interesting because it is the garb and medium of thought and feeling; it is a symbol which has educational value only when it brings us into conscious communion with the things symbolized. All experience is first of all a mental fact. The word "matter," like matter itself, is the expression of a condition of mind.

Culture enables us to see how little worth most of our knowledge has, how little it deserves the name of knowledge. Learn to know and feel the soul of goodness, truth, and beauty, which, however hidden, acts everywhere in man and in the universe, making the world fair and life precious. "There is no easy way of learning what is difficult," says De Maistre; "the unique method is to shut one's door, to say one is not at home, and to work." In education the essential is not programmes and methods, but able and devoted men; not the things taught, but the spirit in which they are taught. To attempt to teach morality as a separate something, and not to recognize that it ought to penetrate and dominate all our studies, is a fatal error. In high men the highest happiness springs from the consciousness of being and doing right. To be truthful and honorable are the most difficult virtues, for truth and honor spring from the finest sense of duty of which the soul is capable. The educator's ceaseless endeavor should be to prevent the formation of habits of wrong-doing; for such habits are enfeeblement of will, are the weakness which is misery. Character is educated will. Will is dark, mind is luminous; and it is the purpose of education to flood the will with intellectual light. What we steadfastly will to be, we become. A mighty purpose gives us now, in a way, what we are resolved to have. It is hardly a paradox to maintain that it is better not to read at all than to read only newspapers. Health and wealth are appreciated when they have been lost; knowledge and virtue when they have been found. He teaches best who enables his pupil to dispense with his aid, as he governs best who makes his rule unnecessary. The virtue of the intellect makes us take delight in truth and beauty simply because they are true and beautiful, as moral virtue makes us love goodness simply because it is good. The shallowness and triviality of man's spirit is the most perplexing puzzle for a serious mind. Since he is not really concerned in any intelligent way, even for his bodily health and well-being, is it not idle to suppose in him a yearning for truth and love? If he takes little pains to make the best of this life, how shall we believe that he truly longs for immortal life? Have we not all, like *blasés viveurs*, lost the sense of the joy and sweetness of life? To see, to hear, to feel, to drink the light of day and star-illumined night, to breathe the perfume of flowers and ripening corn, to watch the pageant of the changing year, the play of children and the flight of birds, to dream, to think, to know, to believe, to hope, to love, — this and all else which only God could give, were bliss and pure delight if we were but sensible of the boundless boon.

"Gods are we, bards, saints, heroes, if we will." The finding pleasure in doing right is a certain result of a habit of right-doing. Immoral conduct is a mark of retrogression toward the life of primitive man; and as savages, when thrown into contact with civilized races, disappear, so in a healthful society there should be an irresistible tendency to eliminate the vicious and criminal. Base pleasures deaden the relish for life. They who are most conscious of the need of self-improvement are most humble, and they who devote themselves most assiduously to this task are most wise. The best men have no price; they can be bought neither with hope of reward nor with fear of punishment, purchased neither with money nor with place nor with pleasure. Let money be thy servant and procurator, not thy lord and master.

Formerly culture was to be had only in half a dozen centres, — in Athens, Rome, or Alexandria, in Paris, Oxford, or Leipsic; but this is true no longer, and when young men tell me they cannot pursue the work of self-education in a Western village, I believe them. The fault lies within themselves. If I have only bread, and you want water, you will go to some one else; if you want muscle and I have only brains, if you want money and I have only virtue, you will not care for me. To have the best of everything is possible only for those who are themselves the best. The best thoughts are to be found in literature, but who loves them? The best eloquence, poetry, and music, like the glories of nature, are wasted merely on clowns and boors. The best which has been made known to man is the power of love, as it is revealed in Christ, but who believes it? Until our faith and knowledge enter into our very flesh and blood, we neither believe nor rightly understand. We truly know only what we have undergone, what suffering has taught us. Over those who lack the spirit of self-sacrifice, ideals have little power; they live in the present, absorbed in the selfish desire of possessing and enjoying. The discipline of want and sorrow by which man has been hammered into shape, purified, and made human, is for them simply an evil. They must indulge themselves; or, if this is denied them they are filled with envy and hate. Knowing nothing of the inner aids to life, they would grasp everything. They do not see that wisdom is taught by suffering, and that consciousness of higher needs is indispensable to the attainment of wealth of heart and mind. Knowledge makes us unafraid, while love ever fills us with dread of loss.

> "Not one but many lives are his
> Who carries the world in his sympathies."

Enthusiasm is a flame which leaps, not from mind to mind, but from heart to heart. It is blown into intenser heat by a single heroic example than by all the proverbs. Whenever a man of genius appears he comes to remain; and whether we love or hate him, he is our master. He who, in utter sincerity, devotes his life to a noble cause — to religion, freedom, science, or art — may be tempted to think, when the end approaches, that he has failed; but such work can no more fail than God can fail.

> To-day of all is best:
> The others are quite dead
> And lie deep in the breast
> Of changeless past at rest:
> Crown, then, to-day thy head;
> To-day be thou God's guest.

What are numbers? One only God makes the universe, one soul may stand against a world, one mind see higher truth than a parliament of nations. Do we not turn from a thousand chattering daws to listen to one nightingale singing to its love alone?

Galileo was thought to be a perverter of religious truth, but when men came to understand him they saw he was a light-bearer through God's heavens. Napoleon, the supreme man-killer, was a poor shot. The secret of power in the world of action lies in the ability to make the many do what even the strongest cannot do himself; but this secret, like that of the poet, is known only to those to whom it reveals itself; it cannot be taught. The sense of power is an essential element in all pleasure, as consciousness of defect is always painful. The highest power is intellectual and moral, and to know that it is ours gives therefore the purest pleasure. The greatest minds and hearts run greatest perils.

Consciousness of defect is the evolutionary principle which urges us toward completeness. In those who feel they know enough, love enough, believe enough, and are all they care to be, this principle is lacking. The finer and deeper the intellect, the keener and subtler is the intellectual conscience, — the love of truth for itself, as being our best equivalent of the supreme reality, the absolute. Contentment with what we have and longing for what we have not are the positive and negative poles of life. Common natures circle about the positive, while the nobler, feeling that this positive is, in truth, negative, reach out for the infinite ideal, which it is impossible indeed to grasp, but which they perceive to be the only essentially real.

> The heart we bear within us makes us men;
> It is the fountainhead of noble thoughts,
> The source of noble living and of power.
> For there is placed the central seat of God,
> Who to the pure and strong of heart gives peace,
> And courage without weakness to endure
> The worst that may befall a guiltless soul.

The higher and purer our happiness, the more peaceful and tolerant we become.

Whatever is, is a manifestation of force. This is the sum of all ideas of being, of that of the absolute even, for God is pure act. "I think, therefore am," is but the affirmation of the identity of force and being. The measure of worth consequently is quantity and quality of power. Nothing distinguishes men of genius from other men so much as their exceptional power of attention. They may not be able to bear a greater weight of thought than others, but they can bear it for a longer time, holding it all the while under the pure light of the mind. The strength of the strong is developed by opposition, by neglect, by threats, and scorn. They know their ability, and indignation at the wrongs they suffer calls it forth.

Our fatal fault is facility. Ten thousand Americans speak, write, teach, govern, and reform the world with facility, but hardly one of us is a master in anything. We are busy with many things, but with ourselves scarcely at all. And we therefore lack the consciousness of defect which impels to the struggle for higher worth. Culture lifts us out of the class in which we were born, for it takes us away from all classes into worlds where only the best live and love. The way is hard and long which, out of the dark prison of ignorance wherein we are born, leads up to intellectual light and liberty; but the goal once reached, the memory of the toil and pain is lost in pure delight. The objections to culture are, at bottom, objections to education; or they are arguments against a partial, superficial, and false cultivation. Like the prejudices of the poor against the rich, they spring generally from envy, from a sense of inferiority, and not from a real view of the aims and ends of culture. Our word "culture" finds its best equivalent in the Latin *humanitas*. It implies a fine humanity, or humaneness, in thought, word, and deed; it is an enlightened and sympathetic consciousness of all that is best in human experience and achievement. It looks away from what is personal and partial, from temperament and whim, from calling and position, from family and people, to what is of universal and permanent interest; and in this world of the universally and permanently interesting, it embraces all things, whether they belong to soul or body, whether they relate to thought or action. That knowledge alone is fruitful which, amid struggle and contradiction, ripens within the depths of one's own heart and is made part of his very being, — is, indeed, himself. Coincidences and harmonies between different nerve-centres of the brain, which have been established by education, may disappear through disuse; but as steeds, turned loose to graze, when taken in hand again, quickly strike the gaits to which they have once been trained, so the channels of habitual thought are never wholly obliterated, but, at the worst, they are choked with a kind of mental drift, which a flood of fresh ideas will carry away. In the highest poetry there is a two-fold life,— that of men and deeds as they stand forth in history, and that which genius pours in and around them; and, since life begets life, this kind of poetry has supreme educational value. To understand a poet, we must feel in reading him the emotion which inspired his song. His words are set to melody, and the music reveals their meaning.

> Best happiness is health of heart, and mind
> Which in sound body works to worthy ends;
> This is the soul of life,— this makes a man,
> And gives to all his being a God-ward trend.

The true view of life is the religious; for no other explains our aspirations and longings, or justifies enthusiasm and self-sacrifice.

The worst consequences of the newspaper habit may be seen in the young, for whom each morning, like a daily meal, accounts of vice and crime are served up, to make them incapable of admiration, reverence, and awe. What father employs burglars, murderers, and adulterers, or quacks, liars, and sophists, as tutors for his children? A man's daily reading, like his habitual conversation, is a symbol of his life and character. To one who was presented to him, Socrates said: "Speak, that I may see thee." Now he would say: "Show me what thou readest, that I may see thee."

> "Most readers, like good-natured cows,
> Keep browsing and forever browse;
> If a fair flower come in their way
> They take it too, nor ask, 'What, pray?'
> Like other fodder it is food,
> And for the stomach quite as good."

To free ourselves from the rudeness of our early manner and speech is comparatively an easy task; what is difficult is to clear the mind of prejudice, and to purify the heart from greed and sensuality. Galton says that not more than one in four thousand may be expected to attain distinction. It is to this chosen one among the thousands that philosophers, poets, and educators always look; and some of them believe that, as there is a love which may create life under the ribs of death, so genius may evoke, with almost miraculous power, thought and desire even from the most unpromising sources. When a nation's thinkers and poets, heroes and saints are all dead, the best part of its life is with the dead.

He who is born to lead finds followers, for nearly all men are born to follow. There is radical wrong in the education which diminishes or weakens the freshness and vigor of the youthful mind and body. The best work the student does is that which teaches him the love of work. Zeal lacks discretion, and a zealous teacher may easily overdo his task, just as an anxious mother spoils her child with too much care. It is with schools as with doctors. If the patient get well or die, we praise or blame the physician; if the pupil succeed or fail, we accredit it to the school, though the cause lie elsewhere. In the things of the mind that which is decisive is not the length of time, but the concentration of power with which we apply ourselves. "The writing of a single page," says Jean Paul, "stimulates the desire to learn, more than the reading of a whole volume." Work to satisfy thine own nature, thine innermost craving for truth, beauty, and love, — not to please another. Should it occur to thee to think thyself worthy of higher honor or place, recall to mind the great poets and philosophers who have lived and died poor and neglected by the world, but "by their own spirit deified."

Failures, for those conscious of inner power, are like trumpet-calls to rally to renewed attacks.

He who has a few facts and arguments at his fingers' ends, thinks highly of his learning, as a well-dressed fellow with a few dollars in his pocket feels rich; but a man of real culture gives little heed to his mere facts and arguments, as one of real wealth hardly knows what he has on or in his pocket. To know one thing thoroughly, it is necessary to know many things; but the one thoroughly known is decisive, is the test of one's intellectual grasp. Accuracy is a result of the habit of observation and attention. Variety and wealth of vocabulary indicate range of thought and degree of culture. When to appreciate an author it is necessary to take a special point of view, he will, at the most, prove interesting only for a few. A fair knowledge of some other language than one's mother-tongue liberates from the bondage of words.

A true teacher is a pioneer through the tangled forest, a shepherd who leads to wholesome pastures, a guide who shows the most practicable road, a physician who tells what diet best suits, a captain who inspires the confidence which is half the battle, a friend who makes the long way seem short. He has himself become and achieved all that he would have his pupil accomplish and be. His example is of more value than many lessons, and to know him and to live in his presence is joy and enlightenment.

How does not intoxicated youth," says Jean Paul, " hang, like bees on flowering lime-trees, drinking in the spirit of a celebrated teacher." A coward makes a coward; a dullard, a dullard; a liar, a liar. Alexander risked drinking poison rather than suffer the poison of distrust. "Heavens!" says Jean Paul again, "how is it that always we find something good in books on education, and so seldom anything of it in teachers?" Not what the teacher says, but what he is and does, draws the young brood after him. I remember how I went on in happy, healthful ignorance until I was eight years old, taught only to look forward to the school as to some Fortunate Isle where Wonderland would be shown. I have not been disappointed.

The teacher's confidence in him gives the pupil confidence in himself; and self-confidence lies at the root of all achievement. It gives strength, and invites help from others; it is half the wisdom of life. To arouse the educational sense is better than to teach rules; for this is the living fountain from which rules have sprung. "The difference between good and bad teaching," says Freeman, "mainly consists in this, whether the words are really clothed with meaning or not." To do any right or useful thing is better than to have the fame of Cæsar. Let neither thy own nor thy party's success lead thee astray, by filling thee with a love of ease or with self-complacent thoughts. Love truth; every lie is a lie to God, and he alone is truthful who shrinks from a lie as an honest man shrinks from a theft. Reverence for all goodness is the fragrant flower and ripe fruit of a noble life. He who has not learned to find pleasure in the good of others is not only uneducated, but uncivilized. As we learn to control nature by obeying her laws, so we learn to govern ourselves and others by obedience to the laws that make us men. Solon, when asked how wrong-doing in the State could be prevented, made this reply: " By teaching those who are not wronged to feel the same indignation at wrong as the sufferers themselves feel." If a merchant, sell honest wares; if an author, write honest truth; if a preacher, speak honest faith. Sincerity is the virtue God and men most love. Let thy ceaseless aim be to gain strength, to develop strength, to preserve strength, — strength of body, strength of mind, strength of will. If thou art a gentleman thou wilt be kindly, modest and brave, sincere and gracious. "No true luxury, wealth, or religion," says Ruskin, "is possible to dirty persons." Behavior, it may be said, is the all in all. It is conduct and more than conduct. It is what poetry is to truth, what style is to thought — it is the fine flower and fair body of noble and righteous life. He who can not behave has no claim on our attention, no right to appear at all. The reward the lover of culture seeks, is the having a cultivated mind, as the reward the lover of God hopes for is the having a godlike soul.

> "That I to-morrow shall be alive
> I frankly do not know;
> But if to-morrow for me arrive,
> That I to-morrow shall fearless strive,
> Beyond all doubt I know."

"Who shootes at the midday sonne," says Sir Philip Sidney, "though he be sure he shall never hit the marke; yet as sure he is he shall shoote higher than who aymes but at a bush."

## CHAPTER II.

### VIEWS OF EDUCATION.

*I seek not to make men read, but to make them think.* — MONTESQUIEU.

THE ear is made for the thrill of pulsing air, but it is fashioned in the silent chamber of the womb; the eye's home is the luminous ether, but it is formed in darkness; and the mind which receives all messages from the outer world, all intimations from the inner, and weaves them into the rich harmony of truth and beauty, gains this divine power in solitude, in lonely dreams and uninterrupted meditations, far from crowds and the noisy contests of vulgar ambition. The highest natures are the most responsive, not only to what speaks to the soul, but also to what appeals to the senses. He who takes genuine delight in life finds the secret of fresh thoughts and inspired words. The physical universe is a school, the State is a school, the Church is a school, life is a school, and in all actual or possible schools, the soul is still its own best teacher. To live and work in the hope that it shall be well for those who follow us that we have lived, is to breathe the bracing air of health and happiness; but this faith is possible only to the unselfish and brave. Morality is the victory of man's higher nature over his lower. The mark of the lower is that it looks to self; of the higher that it looks to God and all things. A nation's power and wealth is never so well employed as in promoting right education. Love of truth is the basis of character. Some emphasize love, others truth; but neither, parted from the other, suffices. No truth has worth unless it be associated with something we love; no love is real unless it be grounded in truth. Sensation is a treadmill, thought leads to new worlds. Whatever widens and enriches life, whatever emancipates the soul, is good.

As the fairest fruit-tree is chiefly wood, breaking only here and there into fragrant blossom and luscious meat, so even the best books are mostly dull matter, where, at intervals, heavenly truth, kissed by the sun of genius, buds and flowers into perfect form. The original thoughts and words of the most inspired author, a little volume will easily contain.

The Philistine thinks lightly of a work of genius, though in some thousand millions of men, there was but one able to do this work.

Whoever is able to do what is worth doing, and able to do it better than any one else, may, without misgivings, set to work. Accomplishment makes cavil absurd. In seeking to raise men above the spirit of the age, let us not lose sight of what is strong and beneficent in this spirit. They who diffuse truth and love belong to a higher race than conquerors and shopkeepers. It is with books as with men, — it is easiest to acquaint one's self with those least worth knowing. Plato will no more speak to the dull and heedless from the printed page than he would have stooped to their level had he met them in his Attic grove. "Privileged minds," said Frederick the Great, "take rank with sovereigns." Nay, they outrank them, just as a real man makes a merely titular personage ridiculous. The impulse to deliver one's self from scorn is a motive not less powerful than the love of praise. Hence poverty or physical deformity is often a stimulus to exercise of mind. Amid the noise critics and readers make about reverberant names, from some obscure corner or the gloom of a prison cell a Milton or a Pascal, a Goldsmith or a Bunyan, a Cervantes or an À Kempis, steals in with his little book and is immortal. Like men, books have their fortunes, but circumstance cannot make what is excellent worthless or what is worthless excellent. Popularity is won and kept by a noise of words, and when the name is no longer sounded it is forgotten; but what the best minds once approve the best minds will always approve. He who finds his pleasure in the mind has what pleases ever with him. The thinker is never lonely, as the lover is never poor. The best legacy a man can leave is a good book. Emerson thought nothing so much wanting in our colleges as a professor of books. It is as difficult to teach the young to know books as to know men. What is best in literature, as in life, is seen to be so only by those who have made themselves worthy of the heavenly knowledge. Richard de Bury says of books: "They are the masters that instruct us without rods and ferulas, without hard words and anger. If you approach them they are not asleep: if you interrogate them, they conceal nothing: if you mistake them, they never complain: if you are ignorant they will not laugh at you."

Books console us for the world of men. Now that printed sheets are scattered fast and thick as snowflakes from wintry skies, who may hope to write aught that shall endure? If any one, he who utters sweetest truth in fewest words.

> We live within the mind and heart alone,
> And whatsoever is not there, for us
> Need not exist: and therefore we may find
> Or make a home in every place and clime,

>    And be ourselves the same, though all else change:
>    For we are what we know and love, and not
>    The things that strike upon the outer sense.
>    So even we may live beneath the eye
>    Of God and dwell in His eternity,
>    While hurrying time with all its roaring sound
>    Sinks into nothingness. But truth and love
>    Remain always, and we also with them.

Like a setter afield, be all alive, with eye and ear and nose, to catch whatever message may be borne to thee from God's boundless game-park. The mind is tinged with the colors the eye habitually rests upon, and there is an unsuspected relation between our habits of looking and our habits of thinking. It is easy to speak ill of books, the best of them being imperfect enough, but they alone bring us close to the thought and love of the greatest and noblest who have lived. It is hard to meet with a superior man, and when he is found he will not tell his secret; but we are forever in the company of God, and in the books of men of genius the best that is known lies open to us. What innumerable lamps night after night are set aglow to illumine the shrines which hold the thoughts of genius, and what devout eyes bend over them and find therein light for the mind, refreshment for the heart, and solace for the soul. Thy days are few, O man of genius, more brief it would seem than those of other men.

Work, then, while time is given thee; clothe truth and love in words which for ages shall be as full of cheer and comfort as the thought of hearthfires to travellers who through the darkness of wintry nights turn their faces homeward. Thy gifts are fatal, but thou wouldst not exchange them for empires.

The more we live within the mind, the more our thought and love take root in eternity: for the soul floating in the awful stream of matter where all things flow on and change ceaselessly, fastens its view upon what is forever the same; and hence when we are truly awake we find ourselves in an ever during and infinite world. As the diver who wearies not will at last bring up a priceless pearl, so the tireless thinker who plunges into the ocean of being will be rewarded, at the least, by glimpses of truth. Wait for a thought, as a fisher for a bite. The curiosity of the noblest minds to learn what cannot be known would seem to be morbid. They still seek what they feel can never be found. But is not this bent of the soul an evidence rather that we are born for God, for eternal life? Dead hopes and vanished dreams, fallen races and mouldering ruins lie along the way of progress. Whoever advances leaves behind something that was dear. But why regret illusions which had power to lead us astray? The loss increasing knowledge brings is gain.

When we cease to learn we cease to be interesting. To learn is to teach one's self; for whether we gain intellectual power and knowledge by observation, by reading, or by listening, the result is the outcome of our self-activity. We are self-taught, and the educator does best when he awakens interest and attention, keeps his pupils mentally alive, makes them as eager to exercise the mind as lusty boys are to run or ride or swim. It is his business to set them thinking. Thousands can tell what they know, but few can rouse to energetic and persevering activity. In a more enlightened age the teacher's chair will be refused to whoever lacks the power to awaken interest. All is wrong when able men are busy with questions of finance, and the training of human beings is left to dolts and dullards. The information the teacher imparts may be had in any encyclopædia, but the impulse to thought and love can be given only by a living soul.

Hast thou sometimes seen a foolish dog rush, with furious barkings, from a farm-yard to attack a train? Such is the wisdom of those who growl at the nature of things, or who would arrest the widening and deepening consciousness of the human mind. Whoever loves may hate, whoever thinks may doubt, whoever is free may fail. This is a permanent condition of human life, which, whatever changes science and progress may make in man's environment, will continue to be the law of his existence. It may happen that the more a thing is proved, the less it is believed. We believe in God before we are capable of understanding what proof means, and no force of argument can strengthen our faith.

Sometimes when I read a line of Horace or Virgil, a sense of pleasure, as from the fragrance of moist woodlands in spring, overcomes me, and memories of my college days start to life like the bursting of buds and the songs of birds. The more life we have, the more we feel that to be alive is a good and happy thing. Pessimism is born of waning vitality, of lack of faith, hope, and love. Love clothes the very body of the beloved with beauty and sacredness; it is the soul throwing itself like a veil about the flesh; it is purity and reverence. Its worship and adoration spring from itself without thought of good or evil. They who have more faith in majorities than in God and the soul do not know what truth and freedom are. To wish that the crowd agree with us is evidence of bad taste, it is a mark of vulgarity. Truth cannot be fitted to the mind as clothes are fitted to the body; it is not the conclusion of a syllogism, but the result of a habit of listening and observing, of doing and thinking. Fortunate are they who have learned to love to do what they ought to do. The desire for what we lack makes us men. "Few friends," says Landor, "fewer acquaintances, no familiars." A great part of wisdom consists in knowing how to get along with fools. Great truths are never perfectly luminous. As the uncertainty of the hour of death gives zest to life, so the obscurity which envelops our highest thoughts adds to their charm. What is manifest is uninteresting. Our very bodies require the mystery of drapery to prevent them from becoming vulgar. The suggestion rather than the revelation of the Infinite is the characteristic of high art. "The naked truth" is a mistaken phrase, for truth to be known must be clothed. The baser metal is the jewel's foil. The fine air of pure truth is too rare for our breathing. The divine thoughts and inspired words of Plato or Shakespeare would never have made their way in the world had they not been imbedded in a grosser element of trivial ideas and vulgar interests.

What the great number of intelligent and enlightened minds accept is but another name for truth. The infinite reason is revealed in the consent of those who know and think. The best work of genius is unintentional,— not what it sets itself to do, but what inner necessity drives it to do; and it is only when it thus utters itself that it is creative. Events solve the great problems, and our discussions and contentions are but the foam that crests the wave. In the world of ideas, the multitude hesitate and are as unsettled as children who give fantastic shapes to clouds. Truth for them takes the form given to it by vivid imaginations, and while they assent, they doubt whether they see what the cloudgazer points out, or they are undecided whether it is like a whale, or a lion, or a human being. The cloud, indeed, keeps no shape, and the view the common mind has of the ideal world is a view of what is ever changing and dissolving.

Women are aristocrats, and it is always the mother who makes us feel that we belong to the better sort. He who lives within lives with God, and needs no other friend. This is the sum of Christ's life and teaching, the divine wisdom of which the world still fails to comprehend. The master need not sign his name; it is uttered by his work. It is not worth while to live if life bring not higher knowledge and purer love.

If he is fortunate who, whenever it pleases him, may call together the most select company, what shall we say of him who, at any moment, can summon from every age and every land, their choice spirits, and hold converse with them as their equal? Is he not among mortals an immortal? Does he not live in serene and enduring worlds, to which nor strength of body, nor beauty, nor youth, nor wealth, nor kingly power can lead? The fundamental precept of pedagogy is this: Study things rather than words, which are but the symbols of things. "Words," says Hobbes, "are wise men's counters,— they do but reckon with them,— but they are the money of fools." The animal hardly distinguishes between itself and the external world, and the thoroughly conscious mind knows that such distinction is largely illusory. Sight, whether of the eye or the mind, makes objections ridiculous. Reason is God's noblest gift, and to discourage its use, whatever the pretext, is impious. The mere intellect is perverse; it takes all sides, maintains all paradoxes, and comes to understanding only when it listens to the whisperings of common-sense. It is the true *enfant terrible*. In the individual, self-consciousness is awakened by self-conscious man; in the race, it is awakened by God. The supernatural is God and the soul. It is better to give than to receive, for giving makes us generous, and receiving makes us helpless. He who has done honest work may die with hope. A new thought consoles us for a day which else were lost. Though we fail, we shall help the universal cause, if we strive under the impulse, not of a party, but of God. The more we fall back upon the inner source of life, the truer our thoughts become. The first and highest need of man is faith in the worth and goodness of life and the source of life. To understand the foolishness of the people, study popular men. Sad infirmity of the thinker and the poet,— they resent the criticism of those whom neither intellect nor imagination controls. The worth of the gift lies in the heart of the receiver. There has been a time when the thought of a game of marbles awakened in me a more pleasant expectancy than could anything now which pope or king or people might promise.

Infinite riches and variety belong to life, and if all seems vain and unprofitable, life's source is running low. To imagine we could do some worthy thing if we but had a proper field is the mark of imbecility. Are not God and his universe with thee? Be true to thy better self, without thought of what purpose thy word and deed may serve. To be weak is to be miserable, but to be strong is not necessarily to be happy. In the right mood the opaque earth seems to become transparent; in the wrong mood the soul itself is but dull matter. If our thought and love were great enough the universe would drift in the line of our desire.

The mark of a cultivated mind is ability to look at all things from an impersonal standpoint, to lose sight of itself and to see with the eyes of others and of God. Only the noblest souls feel how impossible it is to be wholly sincere and loving, to attain to the ideal which is perfect truth and love. Upon those who give themselves through a lifetime to high and noble aims, the shadow of their light at least will fall. The wish to be left alone, to be lost sight of, is thought to be insincere, but only by those who live in the transitory rather than in the abiding world. The unhappy, if they are noble, are often the noblest; for their misery ceaselessly drives them to self-development. When we grow weary of an occupation, a place, or a friend, it is of ourselves we are weary. We seek new surroundings, but what we need is a new self. Thrift is a virtue we all praise. The thrifty succeed; they gain wealth, place, and honor; that they generally unfit themselves for knowledge and the rational enjoyment of life seems to be a minor thing. The aim and purpose of nearly all men is to improve, not themselves, but their circumstances, and so long as this is so there is no hope of any real improvement at all. A blow in the prize-ring sets millions to reading and talking, but after a month it is forgotten; a stroke of the pen passes unnoticed, but after a thousand years it may still be an impulse to noble thoughts and deeds.

"Other delight than to learn I know not," says Petrarch. The best any one may know of life and literature lies open to all, but in the presence of the highest truth and beauty the multitude are indifferent or incredulous. Genius is attention; it is a mind held to the contemplation of truth and beauty with a fascination like that the fairest objects exert upon the eye. It exists to reveal God's thought to the world, and its most favorable environment is poverty, opposition, and solitude. If thou desirest the approbation of fools, be foolish. He who holds no responsible position, but is simply a looker-on, has a reserved seat at life's spectacle. Let him learn to see things as they are, and to make authentic report. The only interests worthy of the serious attention of a lover of truth are those of the mind. Literature is the result of a personal view of things, and science, therefore, can never, in the strict sense, be literature; that is, it can never be a subject of the profoundest interest to man. The mere sequence of phenomena concerns us little; what does concern us is the relation of the whole to our own life, and this is the proper business of literature. The impulse to higher and freer life is given by individuals, never by the crowd, who are always swayed and dominated by the lower needs and common instincts. Profound books are not popular, not because they are hard to understand, but because only a few take genuine interest in the questions which underlie every theory of being and of life. The many are content to see and hear, to taste and touch, and what is beyond is for them as though it did not exist. And when one driven by irresistible impulse takes ultimate problems in utter seriousness, he is misunderstood and called irreligious for being religious. Thought cannot compass thee, O God, words cannot name thee. We can but adore with boundless yearning, knowing thou art above, beyond, and in all, the all in all of every soul that thinks and loves. Only an habitual student can exercise an intellectual influence; only an habitual meditator and holy liver can exercise a moral and religious influence. To teach the child religion is doubtless a difficult task, but in the right environment it will insinuate itself into his life, to elevate his thoughts, widen his sympathies, and purify his desires. "Learning," says Fuller, "hath gained most by those books by which the printers have lost." He is a wise man who uses even the most trifling happenings in his daily life for his own improvement. For purposes of education a true man is worth more than all manuals, codes, systems, and apparatus. Better listen to Socrates on a street corner than to Dryasdust in a marble palace. Repetition is nature's secret. Keep on, and how far thou shalt go, only God knows. The most moral thing in nature is fidelity to fact; change a word, add a line, and if there is an eye to see it is patent. What form genius shall take, God alone can determine; but whatever form it take, men will be grateful.

Occupations which deform and stiffen the body Aristotle calls crafts, and by the same word he designates all money-getting pursuits, because they preoccupy and degrade the intellect. The highest man, he says, finds his pleasure in the noblest things.

"The Ephesians," says Heraclitus, "cast out Hermodorus, the worthiest man among them, saying: 'No one of us shall be worthiest, or let him be so elsewhere and among others.'" Development of faculty is the educator's aim and end, the imparting of information is incidental and subsidiary. The making education free weakens the sense of responsibility in parents. There is a restless activity in the breast of youth, and he is the best educator who turns this energy to high and generous ends. In pursuing our personal aims we run in the dark; when we seek nothing but truth and love, God's light shines about us. I buy many books, and at rare intervals find one worth more than I paid for all the others. These are the pure metal in the mine which consists for the most part of clay and rock. The newspaper is the sewer of average opinion. It is well this should have issue, but when we drink or bathe we seek pure fountains and clear streams. Say boldly what thou holdest to be true; however mistaken, thy thought and speech will not upset God's world. Seek not what thou mayst do, but seek the spirit from which all true work proceeds. What we feel, not what we think, determines conduct; doctrines which have no power to inspire emotion have none to impel to action. We may educate ourselves in every direction; and they are not the least wise who strive to learn the secret of simple cheerfulness. Who shall teach men to find their pleasure in what strengthens, refines, and enlightens? Idleness, ennui, listlessness, trifling occupations, and frivolous amusements consume the time, which, rightly used, would make us all strong, wise, and happy.

The memory of our purest and noblest joys remains with us like a fountain of perpetual youth, while that of the wrong we have done is the only pain which follows us with unrelenting persistence. "The fool," says Confucius, "complains because he is unknown, the wise man because he does not know." It matters little what our special studies may be, if the issue is mental cultivation and moral worth. An elephant that has lived a hundred years has had less of life than a boor who has lived but fifty, and the boor of fifty has had less of life than is given to a poet within an hour. "Glory is so sweet," says Pascal, "that whatever it is associated with, though it be death itself, seems desirable." Acquaintance with the best spoils everything else. We can never make the world of thought a world of facts. Since, however, the world of facts is everywhere and at all times unlovely, they are fortunate who learn to live habitually in the high regions which only the mind can inhabit. Books are an ever present opportunity to turn each idle or weary hour to profit or delight. "The soul of a people," says Voltaire, "dwells in the few who employ, support, and govern the multitude." Let us say, rather, in the few who inspire, enlighten, and guide the many.

Strength and energy are not the same. The energetic are often weak; and the strong, because they are restful and self-contained, seem to want energy. The American has too much energy and too little strength. He is hurried, and lacks the repose which is the sign and symbol of strength. Not what happens, but the way in which we take what happens, is decisive.

The scholar among his books is in paradise, the swineherd is happier among his pigs. Take information from whoever can give it, but follow thy judgment. "He who first praises a book becomingly," says Landor, "is next in merit to the author." He who utters a truth with new depth and intensity makes it new, though the doctrine be old. Is it not a divine privilege to speak a word, to write a phrase, to do a deed, which one's fellow-men shall never be willing to forget? Those who love us understand us better than those who hate. Let us take courage, then, and not think too meanly of ourselves. "Those who trust us," says George Eliot, "educate us." A people's importance lies not in its numbers or its wealth, but in the contribution it makes to the higher good of mankind. If we talk often with a man of profound and vigorous mind we come to see things in the light in which they appear to him; and if we make ourselves familiar with a great book into which he has put the best of his life, we shall be transformed into his likeness in a yet more effectual way. Love divines the destiny of the beloved, and while it points to the rugged way which leads to high achievement, inspires the courage to walk therein with as fresh a heart as though it were some flowery path, illumined by the light of Beauty's eye. They who know and love are able to render the best service. Gifts leave us what we were, but whoever loves and teaches us bestows new and richer life. Perfection consists in realizing the completest accord among the variety of fully developed endowments. The loving heart, the thinking mind, the glowing imagination, the commanding conscience, all acting with freedom and with power, form the pure light of a perfect human life. What is so wonderful as a plastic soul, which, coming into this world of fatal laws and fixed forms, moults its wings and, taking new flight, looks on the whole as though it but now created its universe?

When the high hope and thought of youth remain real and living in the mature man, the result is a great and noble character.

Believe in no triumph which is won by the loss of self-respect or the deadening of faculty. There is no formula for the discovery of truth. Genuine life is life for others. The faith, the hope, the love, the joy, the strength which we impart thereby first become truly our own. The strongest cannot always soar: the eagle himself stoops to earth for food and rest. All work and no play is the dullard's way. The more men think, the less will they agree; but it is more important that they should think than that they should think alike. Questions of money separate husband from wife, brother from brother, and friend from friend. They make all men suspicious and less loving, because questions of money are questions of life, — they mean labor, self-denial, endurance, the long and hard struggle for independence, for the possession of what keeps us from beggary, from sneers and taunts and kicks. Envy, resentment, and hatred are painful feelings, and if virtue permitted us to entertain them, wisdom would forbid. The saddest truth is better than the most pleasant lie. In the best poetry is found the most perfect expression of the purest truth. Truth is most honored when 't is matched with deeds. The most useful things are those which make life good and fair. He who is familiar with the best that has been written thinks modestly of himself; he does not mistake his crotchet for a panacea, or imagine that irritation is enlightenment.

The dogged will to excel effects its purpose. The intellect which analyzes and weakens all else is powerless in the presence of feeling; what we truly love is our very life and resists the destructive force of the critical faculty.

The mind is drawn out and made capable of knowledge when it is aglow with emotion, as the smith forges the metal into shape when it is at white heat. From every flower genius sucks its sweet, but bears within itself the power to make it honey.

There are books whose disappearance would impoverish the whole race. Keep striving; God alone knows what sweet and helpful work thou mayst be appointed to do.

> "In nature there's no blemish but the mind,"
> No beauty but the mind doth make it fair.

Good fortune is the happy ordering of circumstance, making knowledge and virtue easy. In the company of noble minds we grow strong and serene. Power to think is like a mother's breast — the more it is appealed to, the more abundantly it yields. Where emphasis is needed the writer has failed; emphasis is vulgar. The superlative is false style. The secret of style is high thought and pure feeling. Right expression of true thought is final. "Ideas," says Rivarol, "make the round of the world; they pass from tongue to tongue, from century to century, until they clothe themselves in a living and luminous phrase and become the patrimony of mankind." It takes half a lifetime to learn to know the studies we should neglect. The higher thy gifts, the easier it is for thee to go astray. Agree with thyself; with another, agreement can, at the best, be but superficial. "The temple of literary fame," says D'Alembert, "is the home of the dead who dwelt not there when they were alive, and of a few of the living who for the most part shall be thrust forth as soon as they are dead." Memory obeys the heart; where there is love, there is no forgetfulness. We are worth what our love is worth. The perennial charm of erotic writing witnesses to the feebleness of reason; man's thought circles forever and forever about an animal instinct, meant not for the happiness of the individual, but for the propagation of the race. "Not the morning nor the evening star," says Æneas Sylvius, "is so fair as the wisdom which is learned by the study of literature."

> Rest in thy weary, helpless hour;
> So shall the good have double power.

We can know so little; let us at least not be afraid to learn. He is noble who is inspired by thoughts which mean blessings for men. What is worthless in life and literature, we easily learn to know; what is best only patient labor and long experience will teach us.

Whether education bestows power or merely gives freer and more varied action to original endowments is a question of words. It brings into play faculties which without it do not exist or are in abeyance.

Our highest yearnings mark the degree of

culture we have attained; the rude desire pleasure, wealth, and notoriety, the enlightened long for truth and love.

In the best poetry is found the highest expression of the deepest truth. Socrates looked upon himself simply as one who took interest in noble-minded and high-hearted young men, and the favorite disciple of the blessed Saviour was a pure and generous youth, who has given to the world the deepest insight into the Master's spirit and teaching. The thought of the books I have not read, and which like unknown friends are waiting for me, keeps me young. The ideal of peace, of repose, which Wordsworth calls the central feeling of all happiness, is that of the weak or weary. Strong and eager men prefer almost any kind of existence to the tranquil flow of uneventful days.

Haste is the mark of immaturity. He who is master of his tools and certain of himself knows that he is able, and neither hurries nor worries, but works and waits. As what one can lift or bear depends on strength and training of body, so what one can understand or appreciate depends on vigor and discipline of mind. Thou wouldst pour truth into the hearts of men, but wouldst thou pour water into a sieve? Thy doctrines will be of little help unless the heart and mind be made whole. There are no sadder words than these: whiskey and women. They are the epitaph which should be written on so many thousand tombstones on which only lies are engraved. World-moving ideas spring from single minds and never from the deliberations of many; and the men of genius from whom we receive this deeper insight into the nature of things, dwell habitually in thought with what is permanent, eternal, and infinite. Herbert Spencer utters a caution " against striving too strenuously to reach the ideal." In other words, he bids the young beware lest perchance they become too earnest in their efforts to think highly, to act nobly, to love purely, to believe sincerely and to hope steadfastly. Habitual intercourse with nature inspires the love of life, and it reconciles to death; for everywhere in earth and air, there is fulness of life, content and blest within itself; and when death comes, it comes like sleep to tired children who, having played the whole day long, sink quietly to rest. We cannot have full sympathy with our fellows, if we have none with nature and with lower animals. "Sad, indeed," says Herbert Spencer, "is it to see how men occupy themselves with trivialities and are indifferent to the grandest phenomena, — care not to understand the architecture of the heavens, but are deeply interested in some contemptible controversy about the intrigues of Mary Queen of Scots; are learnedly critical over a Greek ode, and pass by without a glance that grand epic written by the finger of God on the strata of the earth."

He who writes need not, but he who publishes must think of a reader; and his hope is that some of the pleasure and strength his thoughts have given to himself will be communicated to others; for if to him they have not been a source of light and joy, in printing them he is but a coiner and passer of counterfeit money.

# CHAPTER III.

## VIEWS OF EDUCATION.

'T is in the advance of individual minds,
That the slow crowd should ground their expectation,
 Eventually to follow.
                                     BROWNING.

### I.

THE popular idea of education is that it is a process whereby the young are fashioned into money-earning machines. Whether the machine is called an artisan, a merchant, a lawyer, or a physician is of minor importance. The ideal of the State is good citizenship, the ideal of the Church is Christian obedience; but where shall we find a school which simply aims to bring all the scholar's endowments into free, full, and harmonious play? Who understands that man is more than a money-earning machine, more than a citizen, more than a member of a church, being nothing less than a son of God, who is infinitely strong, all-knowing, all-loving, all-fair? Go boldly forward along the path thy inmost heart feels to have been made for thee, nor stop to ask whither it lead. The way is thine, the end is in God's keeping. Education is emancipation; it breaks down the prison walls in which the soul is immured, takes it into the light, and bids it soar through the boundless universe, upborne on the wings of truth and love.

Every organism holds within itself the seed of something better than itself, for the infinite God lives within and broods over all. To remain stationary is hardly better than death; imitation is a kind of servitude; the unfolding and upbuilding of one's own being is life and liberty. Political liberty is not freedom; it is, at the best, but opportunity to make one's self free. An enlightened mind is a sanctuary where no tryant may enter. There the Eternal stands guard. He who leads the mind to new worlds or to new ways of contemplating God and the universe is a general benefactor, whose life-enlarging influence all who think shall feel. The tendency which is in things and times requires the shaping and guiding hand of great personalities to turn it to human purposes and ends. An original force is from God and without inner limitation. Its boundaries can be fixed only by its environment. Repression inevitably turns to evil, and the teacher does best work when he wisely stimulates and directs the energies of his pupils.

The best school is that which best helps the free and healthful development of each one's individual endowments; which best enables the youth to become such a man as God and nature intend him to be, not such a one as another's whim would make him. He whom the wanderer's heart drives to far lands saddens his friends who love to stay at home; he whom a divine thirst for truth impels ever into new regions of thought grieves his near ones whom conventional opinions satisfy. To become an ethical fact, to have moral worth, knowledge must pass into action. When scholars become doers the new order will begin. In the presence of whatever system of thought, ask yourself whether it can be made a rule of life; for life, and not speculation, is the test of truth.

Our educators take advantage of the ignorance and inexperience of the young to draw them away from true ideals. They educate with a view to institutions, and not with a view to the Eternal. Their idea of truth is that it is a conventional something; their God is current opinion. The preservation of institutions can never be the end for which we educate. On the contrary, a right education would form a race which would create for itself a higher and nobler environment than any we know. Individuality of power and culture is the ideal each one should strive to attain. Each soul, worth calling a soul, comes into this world unlike all other souls; and the urgency of God and nature within it cries out: Be thyself, not another. Do the work, speak the word thou wast born to do and speak. God makes each one; the inner voice each one hears is God's; become God's man, and let God's word find embodiment in the air thou coinest into human speech. Be not a machine to utter again what others have said; be an aboriginal soul, alive in God, acting and speaking from out the infinite source of all things. It is not conceivable that God should wish to dwarf or paralyze human activity. Let no lesser power, then, bid us keep reason and conscience in abeyance.

Public opinion is a tyrant, who would make men cowards and hypocrites; and it is so easy to make them cowards and hypocrites. That which dwarfs or darkens our being, though it should bring boundless wealth or endless fame, is simply evil. For what life-period do we educate? Childhood and youth are sacrificed to manhood, manhood to old age, which, for the few who reach it, is made miserable by this vicious philosophy. Strong, free, and joyous self-activity, during the whole course of life, can alone develop high, gracious and noble men and women. Whoever or whatever impedes thought and love is evil. When once we accept repression as a legitimate principle, there is no degradation to which we may not descend. Uniformity and equality are possible only when the play of man's nobler faculties is hindered. Why should we think it desirable to make all men alike, since God makes them unlike, and since the more truly they are alive, the greater their unlikeness becomes? Passion is the surging of life's current, and the effort to weaken or destroy it is an attempt on life. The wise educator seeks not to lessen passion, but to increase the intellectual and moral power by which it may be controlled.

Life is the supreme good, and whatever lowers or impoverishes it is evil. God cannot place himself above truth, and a real mind would not suffer dictation from a parliament of mankind. Live not in a great city, for a great city is a mill which grinds all grain into flour. Go there to get money or to preach repentance, but go not there to make thyself a nobler man. The tendency to place education — elementary education at least — almost wholly in the hands of women is wrong. The educator's secret lies in the power to stimulate, and this power man possesses in a very much greater degree than woman. He is the active, she the passive principle. The result of the social evolution, of the reign of democracy, seems to be the destruction of the finer varieties and the formation of a homogeneous mass of coarse fibre. The making use of human beings as means rather than ends is immoral. In this lies the condemnation of our industrialism.

The decisive inequalities are those of mind and heart. The great dividing line is that which separates the wise from the foolish. All work is like a task set a child; its chief worth lies in the exercise it compels, in the education it gives. The truth we seek, more than that which we possess, rouses and educates our powers. The temper in which we face the intelligible universe, rather than the power with which we deal with its problems, is the test of mental character. Look at the world in the pure light of thy own reason, and not through the medium of books and systems. He whose superiority rests upon inner excellence may say to his fellowmen: Provide for me while I feed your minds and souls. To do work one loves is to be happy. Blessed is he who, having found the highest thing he is able to do, gives his life to the task.

All opinions may be entertained except those which weaken and dishearten. The test of the worth of a living faith in God is the strength it gives, the courage it inspires. The objection to culture is that it opens up a world of delightful views, in which we rest, feeling that action is vain. If our whole nature consciously bathed in the being of God we should not only be purer and holier, but we should have more talent, more genius, more ability of every kind. To believe this is something; to know and feel it is joy, strength, and freedom. To make the mind the mirror of all that is, is not enough; we must blend with all that is, love it, recreate it, and make it our own. They who bring the noblest gifts bring them to men too dull to know their worth; and years, centuries sometimes, pass before the divinely great are understood. An original sinner more readily finds pardon than an original thinker. What we are decides our tastes, — it is well with the mole in its burrow, it is well with the swine in its trough. The crowd are willing to proscribe the culture and virtue which are a reproach to them; their hatred is a form of envy. Men are not equal; and were they so, there would be no hope of better things. The multitude move, and have always moved, in a world of low thoughts and desires; and the few who, daring to be unlike the many, rise to higher modes of life, are the benefactors and civilizers by whom progress is made possible. The doctrine of equality is a prejudice of the weak and ignorant, whose conceit persuades them that none are strong and wise. The best are corrupted and disheartened by the crowd who have neither knowledge nor courage. Whatever the compound the chemical elements are the same; and among savages and barbarians the individual is but an atom, an undistinguished part of a homogeneous mass. Hence the measure of the progress of the individual is the firmness and distinctness with which he stands for himself alone.

The only right opposition to inequality is universal opportunity for the best education. The fundamental law is the promotion of God-given endowments; and in a wisely ordered State there should be those whose office would require them to seek for the best talent, and to give it the best nurture, that no original power might be hindered from unfolding itself. Love of company is a chief obstacle to improvement. We cannot remain alone; and when we are together we bore, stupefy, and corrupt one another. We meet to sink into the lower life of eating and drinking, of gossip and play. To be fit to be alone is the first condition of progress. Another obstacle is the labor to which the multitude are condemned. Their work is like the alcohol and tobacco it enables them to buy; it is a deadening of sensation, a refuge from consciousness, a partial escape from life. Thus the many are bestialized that the few may keep company, eat, drink, and dawdle. Were there now some inspired hero to go through the world reuttering the Psalmist's cry, "In my indignation I said, every man is a liar," the echo from all hearts would be: We know it. But only fools tell the whole truth. Even the pious will never understand that it is better men should lose faith than that a lie be told. He who should stand with perfectly frank openheartedness before the public would now be looked upon as lacking mental balance. He would be like one who, single and defenceless, presents himself to an armed and angry mob.

Is it not the tendency of democracy to make men insincere and hypocritical, since, when the law makes all equal, the able resort to cunning and deceit to assert their superiority? What the barons accomplished by brute force, our successful men reach by smartness. Genius is best sense, and its essential quality is sincerity. It is fidelity to fact, to the thing seen and felt. It is the great educator; and teachers who lack genius do their best work when they bring their pupils into sympathetic communion with the masterpieces of creative minds. When a youth first gives his heart to some hero, who to him seems Godlike, he enters the vestibule of the temple of culture. How many of the best and bravest has not Plutarch made conscious of the divinity within them! The lives of warriors — "of those who waged contention with their time's decay" — are alone worthy to be written. Let popular men sink into oblivion with the populace that made them.

The worth of striving depends not upon the success, but upon the fidelity and perseverance with which we continue to hope and labor. The stayer wins, whether the weapons be brawn or brains. Intellectual insight is the purest ray that falls from heaven, and they who seek to break or obscure its light with the grime and smoke of prejudice and passion are the devil's minions. Knowledge problems are but a small part of education. Man is not pure intellect, — he is life; and life is power, goodness, wisdom, joy, beauty, health, yearning, faith, hope, love, action. Make your man a mere science machine, and what more is he than an animal that measures, weighs, and calculates? When you have told me all that is known about the atoms and stars, you have brought to my notice but lifeless facts, whereas I crave for truth, — truth athrill with life. The perfect man is not merely a knower and thinker, but he is also one who lays hold on life and does as well as he thinks.

The test of the value of learning is its effect upon the conduct of life. There is a right and a wrong faith, but what we believe determines character less than the force and intensity with which we believe. Hope may quicken or may deaden the soul. He whose main hope is that he shall die rich has begun to dig the grave of his nobler faculties. What we yearn for is the test of our civilization. If material ends are our ideals, we are no better than barbarians. When we are unable to believe in the divinity of love, the source of life runs dry within us, and our life withers like a tree whose root has been cut. Love beautifies, hate distorts the object we contemplate. That man is God's son is a noble faith, but one which daily contact with human beings tends to destroy; and they who, in spite of disenchanting experience, continue really to hold this faith, live the life of Christ. The liberty which is favorable to high and heroic personalities is the best. Priceless things alone are good, — genius, holiness, heroism, faith, hope, and love. What has a price has small value. The past was not what it appears to us to have been; the future will not be like anything we can imagine; the present is ours, and we should use it to do the highest which through us is possible.

An encyclopædia is not the book a wise student chooses for purposes of self-culture; a man whose brain-cells are stored with innumerable facts is not the kind of teacher an enlightened educator selects for the training of young minds. The teacher's value lies more in what he is than in what he knows; and book-worms are, as a rule, incompetent educators. The sublimest emotions take us nearer to God, to the inner heart of being, than intellectual views. Hence literature, poetry above all, the child of the exalted moods which the sympathetic contemplation of the Infinite and of nature creates, has greater educational value than science. God and his universe are more than all our facts. Wouldst thou go to the relief of the unhappy? Give them courage, faith, hope, and love, — not money, but a new heart.

In literature and in works of science there is a revelation of the best thoughts and the most accurate knowledge the greatest minds have possessed; but the revelation is for those alone who make themselves capable of receiving it, — from the rest it is hidden. In literature, as in all things spiritual, quality is everything, quantity goes for nothing. A phrase outweighs whole volumes. He who seeks to become wise should have leisure, and often be alone with the noble dead, who for enlightened minds live again as friends and helpers. From the day Alexander crossed the Hellespont to conquer the world until now, superior intelligence and courage have triumphed over numbers. Majorities do not rule; they are but weapons in the hands of a wise and high-spirited or a cunning and corrupt minority. They who feel the need of belonging to the majority know not the infinite worth of truth and love.

The imperfectly educated mind is fond of controversy, as rude natures take delight in quarrels. When a thought comes, fasten it with the pen, as you hang a picture on the wall. Thou art taller than I? I will plant a grain of maize, whose tassel in three months shall overtop my head; but I am more than the stalk. Art stronger? A yearling bull is too, yet I am more than it. Hast higher place? So has yonder eagle on his jutting crag, but mind outsoars the reach of wings.

Art wiser and nobler? I bow to thee and am thy servant; be thou my master. If thy influence be evil, desire that it perish; if it be good, the wise and virtuous will wish it to survive. He whom notoriety intoxicates is a vulgar fellow; the love of fame itself is an infirmity; Godlike is he alone who lives for truth and love. The multiplicity and emptiness of books bring concise and pregnant writing into favor,— as the increase of knowledge, rendering the compassing of it by one man, even in a single science, impossible, drives the learned into specialties. The thoughts which as we write them seem warm and glowing as the heart's blood, look cold and dead on the printed page. They are like guests who still remain when the song and dance are done, when the flowers have faded and the lights are out.

An important end of education is to render us conscious of our ignorance; for this consciousness will impel us to seek knowledge. A new truth which offends our habitual thinking hurts like a blow. It is as when we heedlessly strike the foot against a stone, and grow indignant, not because we were careless, but because it was lying there. Culture alone can overcome this unwillingness to accept unpleasant truths. All things that are done are done in time, and our ill success is often due to the belief that we can accomplish at once what only time can bring about. The best work is done by hard work. All men have the right to know whatever is true, to love whatever is fair, and to do whatever is good; and the aim and end of education is to help them to all this. We all live in the midst of a paradise which might be ours, but which for most of us is hopelessly lost. They who make pastimes life occupations, whatever their titles and possessions, are but vulgar triflers. When an idea or a sentiment takes hold of a people and gains such sway as to impel them to heroic enterprise, it exalts, ennobles, and civilizes; it issues in deeds which mark historic epochs, and remain as imperishable evidence of the creative force of enthusiastic faith in the worth of truth and love. In individuals also the purifying and strengthening influence of persistent devotion to intellectual and moral ideals manifests itself in new power of thought and fresh delight in life.

Suggestion is an educational force of the first importance; for the mind is quick to respond to intimations rightly given, but grows listless and inattentive when truth is made plain. The suggester excites curiosity and sets reason and imagination to work, while the demonstrator puts us to sleep. Prove as little as possible, but set the young dogs on the scent of what you would have them run down. Whatever starts the play of the intellectual imagination is profitable and delightful. The pleasure and instruction we find in a poem or a painting, a building or an oration, are due largely to the power with which they compel the mind to exercise itself. He who provokes multitudes, who forces them to recognize that their conceit is but a form of ignorance, hypocrisy, or vulgarity, is a benefactor, but the adulators of the people are confidence men. Where there is right education the future need not be considered; for each hour brings its reward of fairer and richer life. The maxim "Sufficient for the day is the evil thereof" applies also to the good. Do now the best thou canst do. This is thy whole business, and the rest may be left to God.

II.

It is easy to speak lightly of words, as though they were mere idle sound; but an opinion or a belief which has once gotten itself rightly barricaded behind verbal breastworks, will withstand the onslaughts of armies and of centuries. Writing about books is, for the most part, idle writing; for each one must discover for himself the book or books he needs, and it is sufficient that he know there are but a few that are good. Books are saved from oblivion by quality of thought and style. Without this even the most learned and profound are soon superseded or forgotten; for the learning of one age becomes the ignorance of another; and true thoughts badly expressed pass into the possession of those who know how to give them proper embodiment, just as the story becomes his who tells it best. The best books are praised by many, read by some, and studied by few. The inventor of the telephone sets tens of thousands talking to one another from a distance, but their talk is the same old story they have been telling face to face these many centuries. Never shall mortal make a machine which will teach them to think nobler thoughts or to say diviner things. If the bodily eye needs much training that it may see rightly, distinguish accurately among the myriad forms and colors, how shall we hope, without discipline and habitual effort, to acquire justness of intellectual view, ability to see things as they are?

A man's accidents, such as wealth or position, may give him importance while he is alive; but once he is dead, only what was part of himself, as his genius or his virtue, can make him interesting. The craving for recognition should be resisted as we resist an appetite for strong drink. To look for praise or place is to work in the spirit of a hireling. That alone is good for me which gives me freedom and opportunity to lead my own life, to upbuild the being which is myself. Since human power is limited; that which is spent in one direction lessens the amount which might be used in another. The nerve force the sensualist consumes in indulgence, the higher man evolves into thought and love. Favor rather than opposition hinders development of mind and character. If self culture is our aim, let us be thankful for foes, and deem ourselves fortunate when the world permits us to pass unnoticed. Should God lead me to a higher world and offer whatever I might crave, I should ask for the clearest intellectual insight and the purest love.

Half of all that is printed is harmful, and of the remainder more than half is superfluous. It is a problem whether the daily newspaper will not eventually submerge both intellect and conscience. They who live for truth and love should renounce all hope of financial, political, and social success; for those whose home is in higher spheres are not recognized, and should not care to be recognized, by the dwellers in lower worlds. There is a kind of talent which needs encouragement, but it is of the sort which is hopelessly inferior. A Godlike power thrives most when men are heedless of its presence; and the best work has been done by those who received little praise while they were living, and who cared little what should be said of them when dead. Where the individual dwindles, man becomes, not more and more, but less and less; for man exists only in the individual. Let not thy study be to provide for thy present wants or whims, but to do the absolute best God has made thee capable of doing. Talent is inborn. It unfolds itself, however, only under certain conditions. To provide these conditions is the business of the educator, and whatever else he may do is harmful. He who has gained a higher point of view, looks with a kind of hopeless sadness upon those whose eyes are blinded by ignorance or passion.

In whoever is destined to achieve distinction the spirit of discontent lives like a god. "To accustom mankind," says Joubert, "to pleasures which depend neither upon the bodily appetites nor upon money, by giving them a taste for the things of the mind, seems to me the one proper fruit which nature has meant our literary productions to have." Early ripeness, long life, and youthful-minded old age are the conditions required for the best development of man's powers. They who see things in a new light influence opinion, but mere makers of syllogisms and propounders of arguments speak and write to no purpose. To have value, knowledge must be intelligence, and not merely erudition. It is for the mind, not the mind for it.

The philosopher, poet, or man of science who says he has no time to waste in getting rich, speaks, in the opinion of the crowd, sheer nonsense, though he simply expresses the generally received truth, that what we are is of more importance than what we possess.

As distance seems to bring the stars close together, so in remote epochs great men and great deeds appear to stand thicker. This is but a form of the illusion which perspective always creates, and to which we must also attribute the prevalent notion that in ancient times heroic virtue was less rare than in our own. "In cheerfulness," says Pliny, "lies the success of our studies." We live only as we energize. Energy is the mean by which our faculties are developed, and a higher self-activity is the end at which all education should aim. Whatever else may succeed with us, we all fail in love; and in this lies the essential sadness of life. He who cannot perform noble deeds will not be able to write in a noble style. He who takes interest in a pugilist rather than in a philosopher or a poet is as though he were a dog or a cock. The lack of money may cause discomfort, but the lack of intelligence makes us poor, the lack of virtue makes us vulgar. Lack of money may be supplied, lack of soul never. The money we owe enslaves us, the money we own corrupts us. Whoever can influence men should strive to make them more courageous, more enduring, more hopeful, simpler, more joyful.

"Books," says Emerson, "are the best of things, well used; abused, among the worst. What is the right use? What is the one end which all means go to effect? They are for nothing but to inspire."

There is no phrase more suggestive than this of the Gospel, — to "throw pearls to swine." This is what the makers of literature have been doing from the beginning; and that which still survives as literature is what a few heavenly minds have picked up from beneath the hoofs of the herd, whose uplifted snouts pleaded for swill, not for thought. Descartes and Spinoza, like Plato and Aristotle, hold that blessedness consists in knowing in so living a way that to know is to admire, to love, to be filled with peace and joy. A man of genius is like a barbarous conqueror; he slays the victims he despoils, and so what he steals seems never to have belonged to others.

"The philosopher," says St. Evremonde, "devotes himself, not to the most learned writings to acquire knowledge, but to the most sensible to strengthen his understanding. At one time he seeks the most elegant to refine his taste, at another the most amusing to refresh his spirits." Whoever reads to good purpose seeks to place himself at the writer's point of view. He reads for inspiration and knowledge, not to find fault. There are many whose view of education is that it is a process of taming, like the domestication of animals. They strive to subdue the child and make him pliable to another's will; and when he has become thoroughly tame, they think he is well educated. A tame horse, however, if we consider its own good, is inferior to one that is wild; and whoever or whatever is overcome and made subject is weakened and dispirited. Whatever we teach boys, girls should be taught the science and art of education itself; for three-fourths of them will become mothers, and education is a mother's chief business, in which if she fails, schools and other agencies are powerless to form true men and women.

What gives pleasure is of little moment, what gives power and wisdom is all-important. The degenerate seek ease and comfort; the strong love adventure and danger, hardship and labor. To lead a moral and intellectual life is to make one's self, physically even, attractive.

When the discerning perceive that an author addresses himself to a circle, a party, or a class, they care not what he says; knowing that if it were worth writing, he would utter it simply from his inner being, and without thought of impressing others. A book thrown in our way by chance, an acquaintance made by accident, changes the whole course of life. We are strong when we follow our own talent, weak when another's leads us. Whoever is made free frees himself. This is the meaning of the Gospel phrase: "Ye shall know the truth, and the truth shall make you free." Another may break down prison walls and strike off fetters, but this liberating truth each one must teach himself, or never know it at all. Duration rather than intensity of high and passionate feeling makes the man of genius. The human race is so poor in men of real intellectual force that when it finds one it receives him gladly, whatever his defects or perverseness may be. Whoever impels to high thinking gives pleasure, and of a nobler kind than that which a fair scene or rich wine or delightful company can give. Why should the American who is most alive be able simply to make the most money? Why should he not think the highest thought, feel the deepest love? Sensation lies at the root of thought. We really know only what experience, suffering, and labor have wrought into our very being. Hence the young have no true or deep knowledge.

In educating, as in walking, we have an end in view. In educating this end is an idea, — the idea of human perfection; and to develop and make plain this ideal is more important than any of the thousand questions with which our pedagogical theorists are occupied; for to say we live by faith, hope, love, and imagination is but a way of saying that we live only in the light of ideals. A student wrote this over his door: "Who enters here does me honor, who stays away gives me pleasure." "To read to good purpose," says Matthew Arnold, "we must read a great deal, and be content not to use a great deal of what we read."

A cultivated mind entertains all ideas and all facts with attention, just as a polite and brave man is gracious to all comers. The painter studies the body in nude models. Let the thinker, if he would know the value of his thought, strip it of verbal ornament. The showy dress of words but hides the lack of truth, as a fine phrase makes its content credible. "Not more than one in one hundred thousand of the books written in any language," says Schopenhauer, "forms a real and permanent part of literature."

In literature is preserved the essence of the intellectual, moral, and imaginative life of the best minds. A good book may easily be more interesting than its author; for there we find pure and refined what in him was commingled with baser matter. I cannot read all books, but I can read many; and the writers of the many I read have read all that is worth reading. The journalist is an alarmist. His newspaper sells in proportion to the excitement he succeeds in creating. Wars, disasters, panics, famines, plagues, outrages, scandals, form the element in which he thrives. His readers lose the power to remember, to think. They lose the sense for simple truth and beauty, for proportion and harmony. Like the readers of cheap novels, they become callous, and can be roused to momentary attention only by what is startling or monstrous. The journalist seeks what will make immediate impression; a real mind looks to truth and to permanent results.

No one actually holds within his memory one ten-thousandth part of the information contained in a book such as the British Encyclopædia; and he who knows most of the Encyclopædia is probably a man in whom there is little spontaneity, little of that mental quality which gives one's thought personal, that is real, charm and worth. "Truth that has been merely learned," says Schopenhauer, "is like an artificial limb, a false tooth, a waxen nose; it adheres to us only because it has been put on."

The right to punish implies the duty to teach and educate. Once we have gained insight into life's meaning, we see how nearly all men, like hounds astray, are following scents which lead nowhere. He who writes with care day by day will learn at least how to say things. For the education of men, which is the highest human work, one heroic, loving and illumined soul is worth more than all the money-endowments. How poor are they who have only money to give! May it not be a consciousness of the small value of what they can bestow that hardens the hearts of the rich? They who give money give like those who give food; they who give truth and love give like God.

As the miser lives ever, in thought, with his gold, the lover with his beloved, so the student lives always with the things of the mind, with what is true and fair and good. High purpose and the will to labor mark those who are predestined to distinction. To have knowledge but no skill, no ability to do any useful thing, avails nothing. Herein lies the defect of our education: we are taught everything except how to work wisely, bravely, and perseveringly; how to strive not for money and place, but for wisdom and virtue. Learning without faculty leaves us impotent, and may easily render us ridiculous. In each soul there is a world in embryo, and the teacher's business is to help it to be born. To interest the young in themselves, in the world that is in and around them, that they may realize that its implications are divine, is a chief part of education. The best help is that which makes us reverent, self-active and independent. Work reveals character. We know what a man is when we know, not what his opinions and beliefs are, but what he does or has done. Our highest aspirations reveal our deepest needs. Better be one whom men hate than one whose ideal is good digestion, good clothes, and general comfortableness.

The true educator strives to draw forth and strengthen the sense for truth and justice, and to develop a taste for the purer and nobler pleasures of life. His aim is to make men good and reasonable, not to make them smart and eager for possession or indulgence. The discipline of sorrow, of sorrow of a great and worthy kind, has a high educational value. More than anything else it purifies the sources of life and forms character. Every choice spirit seeks some fortress, some soul-sanctuary, where he may live for truth and God, far from the crowd who neither know nor love. You are not I, your good is not mine. Go forward, then, and prosper; your gain can never be my loss. We thoroughly understand only what we have outgrown. Intellectual progress is an approach to truer estimates of values. A man is what he is and who he is, not by virtue of wealth or office, but by the quality of his thought and life. "Thinking and doing, doing and thinking," says Goethe, "is the sum of all wisdom, — so recognized and practised from the beginning, but not understood by every one."

## CHAPTER IV.

### PROFESSIONAL EDUCATION.

Godlike is the physician who is a philosopher.—HIPPOCRATES.
The philosopher should end with medicine, the physician begin with philosophy. — ARISTOTLE.

AS the whole science of arithmetic is contained in the multiplication table, so the whole significance of life is summed up for each one in his table of values. What has worth and what is the relative worth of desirable things? This is the primal question for whoever has the will to exert himself; for as he feels and thinks on this subject, so will he act. To mistake here involves the drifting of his whole existence away from what is best, from what is true, good, and fair. At first thought it would seem that there are certain fundamental notions as to what is desirable, upon which all agree. Who can doubt, we may ask, that it is better to be than not to be, that what has life is being in a higher sense than what is inanimate, and that the degree of worth in living things is measured by the power and quality of life? But there are men who take no mean rank as thinkers, who call life evil and death good, who hold that it is better not to be than to be, as there are others who prefer ignorance to knowledge, pleasure to duty, strength of body to intellectual power, and material possessions to spiritual insight. To some, it seems good to have many slaves, many wives, many children, while others believe that slavery degrades the owner not less than the owned, that one wife is more than enough, and that desire for children, the result of instinct and not of rational motives, is felt most by those who think least. As men become more intelligent and civilized, they argue, they grow less able and less willing to have offspring, and he who knows what life is, if reason controls him, should be as unwilling to transmit it as to take it.

To most men, wealth and power, position and fame appear to be supremely desirable, and yet there are many who are persuaded that to the nobler sort of life, riches and honor and place and renown are hindrances. Of the worth of friendship, as of that of the love of women, opposite views are taken. Civilization is decried as a state of degeneracy; art, as at once the result and the cause of an effeminate temper; and religion, as the chief source of the worst evils which have afflicted mankind. Thus widely do we differ as to the value of things. The chief barrier between men is not wealth, or rank, or creed; it is opposition of life and thought; for these determine the worth of all things. The mind is the creator of interest and consequently of value.

> See yonder youth and maid how wrapped they are
> each in the other;
> See yonder two white lambs that gently push
> their heads together.

I look and feel a momentary pleasure, but if there is interest, I create it by putting thought in what, in the lovers and the lambs, is but sensation. Life is interpreted by thought, but it is enrooted in faith, which, with the aid of knowledge, supplies the element of value in every sphere of human action, since that alone seems good to us in which we genuinely believe, whether it be money or wisdom, pleasure or power, the world or God. What is anything worth to him who believes in nothing, who is indifferent to all things? What is aught but as it is esteemed? Faith is wedded to desire, and desire gives value. What we yearn for seems to be more truly part of ourselves than what we possess. Hence youth with its longings is richer than age with its millions. Hence religion which makes us conscious of our infinite needs, and utters itself in ceaseless prayer and sacrifice, is man's chief consoler and joy-bringer. Hence genius which feels itself akin to all things, and is impelled to identify itself with all things, is beatified by its own spirit. Hence faith, hope, and love, the triune fountainhead of boundless desire and aspiration, are the springs of life upwelling from central depths of being. The divine joy and goodness which the young find in life are there in truth, and they in whom reflection or experience has destroyed this vital faith, have lost the view of things as they are. Fortunate is the orator who finds an audience whom the all-hoping soul of youth persuades, with an eloquence whose secret words cannot convey, to trust in whatever is high, or holy, or excellent; and still more fortunate is he when those who listen are drawn by an inner attraction to devote their lives to a profession in which to be ignorant is to be criminal.

Belief in the good of knowledge is not the weakest of the bonds which unite the members of the learned professions; for whether our special study be theology, or law, or medicine, or pedagogy, that which determines our place and power to render service is knowledge, and the skill that comes of knowledge. It is expected and required of us that we be the wise men among the people, able to counsel, to guide, and to defend them wherever their vital interests are at stake. Our callings have their origin in human miseries. Disease, folly, sin, and ignorance make physicians, lawyers, priests, and educators possible and necessary; and the infirmities upon which they thrive are so related that he who ministers to one ministers to all. Another bond is thus woven into the very constitution of the liberal professions. Disease, in innumerable instances, is the child of folly, sin, and ignorance; folly, the child of sin, ignorance, and disease; sin, the child of ignorance, disease, and folly; while ignorance may be said to be the common mother of all our miseries. Were there no disease, there would be no physicians; were there no folly, there would be no lawyers; were there no sin, there would be no priests; were there no ignorance, there would be no teachers. It is, then, our unenviable lot to live, like moral cannibals, on the misfortunes and weaknesses of our fellowmen; and it is but natural that we should be made immortal themes of exhaustless satire and abuse. What a general blessing have professional men not been to the whole literary tribe!

The priest's love of ease and power, the lawyer's cunning and dilatoriness, the physician's wise look, and his blunders hidden by the grave, are subjects which must find a ready response in the general heart, since books are full of them. Queen Mab tickles the parson's nose, as he lies asleep, with a tithe-pig's tail, and he dreams of another benefice; she drives over the lawyer's fingers, and he dreams of fees. His clients are like flies in the spider's web.

> "When once they are imbrangled
> The more they stir, the more they 're tangled."

Doctors themselves, I imagine, more than half agree with Macbeth, when he bids them throw physic to the dogs, for he 'll none of it.

> "Physicians mend or end us
> Secundum artem; but although we sneer
> In health, when sick we call them to attend us,
> Without the least propensity to jeer."

If not witty ourselves, like Falstaff, why should we object to being the cause of wit in others? We are sure to have our revenge, for men will still be fools, and sinners, and invalids, and however much they mock, they will call us in the hour of need. It is vain to warn them against priests, lawyers, and doctors,— they will never be wise and never be well.

In sober truth, we are the best friends of man, for we are all ministers of health, without which life is hardly a blessing. Whatever may contribute to the bodily well-being and perfection of man is the physician's concern; whatever may secure individual rights and promote social justice is the lawyer's; the priest's is the soul's health, morality, and righteousness. They all strive for stronger, purer, nobler life, in the body, in the conscience, in the soul, in the individual, in the State, in the Church. Their mission is high and holy, it is Godlike, and to fulfil it rightly, the best gifts thoroughly cultivated are not too great. That which they, day by day with ceaseless efforts, labor to accomplish is the prophet's vision, the philosopher's truth, and the poet's dream; and what else do patriots, statesmen and men of science long for than the kind of life which it is the business of the learned professions to foster? To these high callings no servile spirit should belong. By the common consent of the civilized world they are denominated liberal, for only the free and enlightened mind can grasp their significance or enter with right disposition upon the work they involve. Not pleasure or wealth or the love of ease or any lower motive may open the door of the temple of knowledge and religion; but they who seek admission should feel that they devote their lives to sacred tasks, in which the more they succeed the more shall they have to labor and endure. They should have youth's deep faith in the good of life, and be willing to deny themselves, and to persevere through years in the work of self-culture that they may make themselves worthy to become the bearers of the best gifts to their fellow-men. The prolonged infancy and childhood of the human offspring is nature's compulsion to education, and the noblest minds are conscious of an inward impulse driving them to become day after day, self-surpassed. The doctrine that the individual dwindles, while the race is more and more, they do not accept, for they know the race exists only in individuals, the highest of whom give it wisdom and distinction, glory and strength. From their early years they hear the appeal of the unseen powers whispering to them: Be men, not merchants, or lawyers, or doctors, or priests, but Godlike beings; not means, but ends, for the universe exists that perfect men and women may be formed. An inner voice teaches them that man lives to grow, to upbuild his being, and that effort is the source of all improvement, being nothing less than the hold the finite has upon the infinite. Before they begin the special studies which are to fit them more immediately for the calling they have chosen, they will have gotten a liberal education; for the mind is the instrument with which they shall work, and since the interests to be committed to them are of paramount, nay, supreme moment, this instrument can never be too perfect. Is it conceivable that awkward, undisciplined intellects should rightly apprehend the deep and complex sciences which are the subject matter of the learned professions?

A liberal education is not so much knowledge

as it is a preparation for knowledge. It is openness and flexibility of mind, delight in the things of the intellect, justness of view, candor, patience, and reasonableness. It has a moral as well as an intellectual value. It is discipline of mind and of character. It opens higher worlds than those the senses reveal. It offers nobler aims than the pursuit of material things; it liberates from sordid views and the mercenary mind, and thus establishes the primary condition of genuine success; for each one's worth as well as the worth of what he does should be estimated by the spirit in which he lives and strives. If he take no delight in his work, but labor solely with a view to profit, it is a mere chance if he do not become a criminal. A liberal education does for the mind what wholesome food and healthful exercise do for the body, — it gives vigor, energy, endurance, ease, and grace. As the athlete performs feats which the untrained can only admire, so cultivated intellects accomplish what ruder minds cannot understand or appreciate. There is a quickness of perception, a clearness of view, a soundness of judgment, a power of discrimination and analysis, a sureness of tact, and a refinement of taste, which education alone can give. It bestows also a sense of freedom, that inspires courage and confidence, which are elements of strength, whatever the undertaking be; while the faculty to think, to reason and compare, the ability to see things as they are, which it confers, gives those who have received a liberal education manifest advantages over others in the prosecution of scientific and professional studies. Their knowledge is more accurate, it is more intimately related to life, their mental grasp is firmer, their view wider and more profound. They escape the narrowing influence of purely professional studies, which, if unhindered, would make us mere theologians or lawyers or physicians, whereas it is our business to unfold our being on every side and to make ourselves alive in many directions. Division of labor makes everything cheap,— man first of all; and the increasing tendency to specialization may have the effect, not only to lower the standard of professional life, but to interfere with the development in the professions of strong, many-sided personalities, interesting in themselves, and lending dignity to their callings; who, while they are masters in their several departments, are none the less at home in the whole world of human interests and speculations. The man of liberal education is a lifelong student, and the habitual student is rarely content to think and read but in a single direction; for he soon perceives that all kinds of knowledge are related, and that he who would acquire the full and free use of his intellectual faculties must exercise himself in all the fields of thought. While he acquaints himself with the best that has been thought and written, he will keep pace with the progress of research and speculation in his own profession, for, in the midst of a thousand cares and duties, he will still find time to read and meditate. He will be a thoroughly informed theologian, lawyer, or physician, but he will also be an accomplished man, whose speech and behavior will help to refine and exalt the society in which he moves. He will hold his opinions with firmness and he will express them with ease and grace. His principles will be pure, his sympathies large and his religion unfeigned. A good friend and a pleasant companion, he will be most happy when he is permitted to hold communion with the great minds of all ages, or to retire into the world of his own contemplations. To him no company is so pleasant as that of true and beautiful thoughts; for they are forever fresh and invigorating, and like well-bred people, if we begin to tire, they take their leave, till the right moment return. His professional experience will reveal to him much of the weakness and miseries of men, but his sympathy and love will thereby be purified and strengthened.

While I thus treat of professional life and

education from a general point of view, and somewhat in the spirit of an idealist, I do not lose sight of the occasion which calls forth this discourse. As a minister of religion I should and do take a genuine interest in whatever concerns the science and art of healing. The first priest was the first physician, as well as the first lawgiver and ruler, for government, literature, science, and art all had their cradle in the temple of religion, and were nourished by faith in the unseen powers. Asclepios, the gentle artificer of freedom from pain, was a son of the gods, and from him Hippocrates, the father of medicine, claimed descent. To the religious spirit in which he followed his profession, the oath he prescribed to all physicians that they would pass their lives and practice their art in purity and holiness, bears witness. To come to what concerns us more nearly, the Founder of the Christian faith came not merely as a teacher of divine truth and a savior of the soul, but he came also as a healer of bodily infirmity, and in much of what is recorded of him the restoration of health is a striking feature. At the sight of suffering his sympathies awaken, and care for the sick is one of the virtues he especially emphasizes. The first definite duty he imposed upon his disciples was that of travelling about to announce the Kingdom of God and to heal those afflicted with disease. Of the four who have left record of his life one was a physician. There may be higher things than the alleviation of pain, but there is no more genuine test of love for men, which is a fundamental principle in the life and teachings of Christ. The spirit of humanity which he more than all others has awakened and strengthened, is nowhere better exemplified than in the medical profession as it exists in the world to-day. The true physician waits as a servant upon the miseries of man; like a soldier at his post, he stands ready to bring relief. Neither darkness of night, nor storm, nor contagion, nor pestilence, nor the field of carnage can deter him when duty calls. His service is at the command of rich and poor, and his mind is ever busy with thoughts that bear on the prevention or cure of disease, for with him preventive medicine takes precedence of the curative. In this he obeys the law of Christian charity, for, if to minister to the sick is Christlike, to forestall disease by searching into its causes and discovering how they may be removed is not less a godlike thing. They who throw themselves as consolers and servants into the midst of pest-stricken populations are God's men and women; so also are they who teach us how pestilence and contagion may be excluded. Worthy of praise and imitation are the builders and endowers of hospitals for the poor, but more worthy yet are the educators who show the people how disease may be avoided, and the philanthropists and statesmen who place them in health-giving surroundings. From what unimaginable sufferings has not the knowledge of the prophylactic and therapeutic properties of quinine saved mankind? To what countless millions has not Jenner come with his vaccine, bringing, like a God, immunity from one of the most terrible diseases? Who can estimate the mitigation of pain and the saving of life brought about by the use of anæsthetics?

Aseptic and antiseptic treatment has opened a new era in surgery, enabling the operator to use the knife with full confidence of success in cases which for centuries had been thought desperate. Pasteur, as competent judges believe, has found a preventive of hydrophobia, and why shall we not look forward to the day when the bacilli which cause tuberculosis, cholera and other parasitic diseases shall be under the control of the physician?

It has been shown plainly enough to convince the most sceptical that organisms wholly invisible without the aid of the highest magnifying powers, cause each its particular infectious disease. Men of science have succeeded in cultivating these bacilli like plants in a garden.

They keep them in glass tubes on the shelves of their laboratories and handle them with impunity, and we can not believe that our control over the infinitely small will stop here. When once the cause of disease is clearly known, the human mind which weighs the stars and counts the pulsations of light, will find a remedy. The men who are striving to do this work, often in silence and obscurity, remote from the praise and approval of the world, are carrying on a warfare in comparison with which the noisy battles of history are as insignificant as the shouts and stone-throwings of a rabble. They stand face to face with disease and death in their most secret lurking-places, from which, from the beginning of the world, they have made assault on life. Of old it was affirmed that man's life is a warfare, and the saying has come down to us who find a deeper and more important truth in it than the ancients ever suspected. Apart from the world-wide struggle for existence, in the large and historic sense, each living organism is a battlefield. Consider for a moment the wonderful part which the white corpuscles of the blood play in defence of life. Their work may be studied with the aid of a microscope in the web of a frog's foot, in which irritation has been caused, as the bacillus of disease causes irritation. When the inflammation begins, the white corpuscles lag behind and hug the sides of the veins and arteries; a little later we may observe them passing through the walls of the blood-vessels into the surrounding tissues, and again returning into their natural channels, from which they had issued to attack the organism that had set up the irritation, and to destroy it or themselves to be destroyed. These white corpuscles, then, which are found in the blood in the ratio of one to five hundred of the red particles, move with the life-bearing fluid, like soldiers who guard a convoy and are always ready to repel the enemy. Hence they are called phagocytes, devourers of disease-producing germs. These protoplasmic soldiers are the wisest medical teachers, and the whole profession is beginning to learn the lesson they inculcate, that the best treatment is warfare on the cause of disease. The phagocyte plainly tells us also that the cause of disease is not an imaginary entity or influence, but a real being which, in many cases at least, is a living organism.

There is of course no real break in the history of medicine, but from the time of Hippocrates to the beginning of the nineteenth century, though several important discoveries were made, and new remedies and modes of treatment of more or less value were introduced, the progress of medical science was altogether unsatisfactory. Old theories gave place to new, and new methods were substituted for the old, but the gain was not great. The revival of the study of the writings of Hippocrates and Galen, in the fifteenth and sixteenth centuries, did not produce any important reform. Physicians continued to rely upon authorities rather than on facts. The discovery of the circulation of the blood, made by Harvey in the early part of the seventeenth century, was a significant event, but it produced no immediate effect on the practice of medicine. Faith in the old dogmas was weakened, but belief in the good or necessity of schools and systems survived. The names of Sydenham, Boerhaave, Hoffman, Stahl, Haller, Cullen, Brown and Rush will retain a place in the history of medicine, but their contributions to the science and art of healing have little historic significance. The Vienna school of the eighteenth century deserves recognition for its insistence upon the necessity of carefully studying the facts of disease during life and after death; and also because Avenbrugger, a Vienna physician, was the first to employ percussion as a means of diagnosing pulmonary affections. Thus we approach the modern school of medicine, in which the methods of physical science are adopted, while little importance is given to theories or to hypotheses, unless when they are used as guides in the search after facts. Starting with the assumption that vital phenomena, both in health and disease, conform to laws and are therefore intelligible, the new school, with the aid of new instruments, has created new sciences, which have a more or less direct bearing upon the practice of medicine. The study of organic types, microscopic anatomy, experimental pathology and therapeutics, have brought knowledge where ignorance had prevailed; while auscultation, percussion, microscopy, physiological chemistry, the thermometer, the ophthalmoscope, the auricular speculum and the laryngoscope enable the physician to make diagnosis certain in cases in which hitherto he had been left to surmise. The increasing number of known parasitical organisms, which are the causes of disease, permit him to substitute real for imaginary etiological entities. His view is clearer, his judgment sounder, his treatment more effective for he moves in an intelligible world. His feet are in the way which has led to all the marvellous achievements of physical science. In the presence of forces which are pregnant with life or death, he no longer fights blindly, or with the fatal confidence of the empiric. If he have theories they rest on the basis of facts carefully observed and accurately determined. Medicine henceforth is so guided, surrounded and protected by science, that it can no longer drift with the currents and countercurrents of opinion and speculation. The greatness and worth of the present age lie in its intellectual activity rather than in its material progress. There is in it a mental stimulus as strong as that which impelled the Greeks of the age of Pericles, to produce, in every sphere of thought and action, the works that still remain as an exhaustless source of inspiration. The discovery of America is unimportant and commonplace when compared with the discoveries made by scientific investigators. We live now not merely in a new world, but in new worlds, whose boundaries are enlarging, whose secrets are ever revealing themselves to patient seekers. In the heavens and on the earth we see things never before beheld by the eye of man. The impulse of this movement is necessarily felt by the learned professions. The light which has been thrown upon the past, upon the earliest struggles of mankind to attain a human kind of existence, upon the evolution of languages and customs, upon the primitive conceptions of right, of duty and of law, has made possible a science of sociology which gives us a larger and profounder view of the sphere of man's life. Biology interprets the problems of psychology and psychology provides methods for pedagogy. The comparative study of religions, the more comprehensive grasp of the history of philosophic systems, the criticisims of the Sacred Writings with the aid of philology, anthropolgy and ethnology, the more accurate analysis of the elements of thought and the juster appreciation of the value and import of knowledge itself, have opened new realms to all who love the things of the mind, and, first of all, to those whose office compels them to deal with the problems of the unseen world, with the supernatural, which is God and the soul. In none of the professions has the intellectual movement of the age produced such wholesome and satisfactory results as in medicine. In law and theology the influence of the scientific spirit tends to disturb and unsettle, but in medicine it is altogether salutary. The modern physician, putting aside the old methods as unsuited to the study of vital phenomena, no longer seeks to know what life is, but regards it merely as a natural process, manifesting itself in health and disease; for, if life is health it is also disease, since it inevitably tends towards and ends in death, though no specific malady should intervene to hasten the march to the grave. Death is the correlative of life, as disease is the correlative of health. To think the one is to imply the other. It is the physician's business, then, to acquaint himself with the structure and functions of the body in health and disease. Without a knowledge of anatomy and physiology he cannot understand disease, which is a deviation from the line of normal physiological conditions, whether structural or functional. The theory of disease, however, is but an idle speculation if it lead not to the means of cure; and hence pathology calls for therapeutics, the theory of remedies, which is also a science, for nearly every article of the materia medica produces an effect on the organism which may be ascertained with scientific precision. But when there is question of adapting remedies to diseases the wisest physicians recognize now more than ever before that they enter an obscure region where they feel rather than see their way. The best doctors give least medicine, and they would give less if their patients were not persuaded that the most certain way to frighten death is to keep swallowing poison. The practice of medicine then is still, to a great extent, traditional and empirical, and however wide and profound the physician's knowledge may be, he soon learns that ceaseless vigilance and attention to innumerable details can alone keep him from becoming a murderer. Hahnemann and his disciples have doubtless rendered service by showing how well the sick may prosper by taking, at brief intervals, a sugar pellet or a teaspoonful of water.

Physicians more and more insist upon the importance of regimen and diet, of pure air and healthful occupations, upon sufficient sleep and rest, upon cleanliness of person and surroundings. They know that, in innumerable instances, disease is the result of careless, ignorant, or vicious habits, that function and appetite are correlative, and that excessive indulgence perverts the action of the organs which insure the harmonious play of the vital forces. They know that diseases have definite causes, and that it is their business to keep these harmful agencies away from those who are well, and to help nature to expel them from those who are ill. With the increase of knowledge the scope of all the professions is enlarged, and we may now no longer look on the physician as simply a healer or an assuager of pain. It is his business to understand the laws of hygiene and sanitation, to acquaint himself with climatic conditions, to know the kinds of dwelling, clothing and diet, which are most favorable to health. He should, in a word, as his title of doctor implies, be a teacher. The homely proverb that "an ounce of prevention is better than a pound of cure," which has given rise to many maxims and observances more or less salutary, he should be able to interpret and apply in the light of scientific knowledge. There is no country in which such teaching is more needed than in our own, or in which it might be given with stronger hope of good results. America, it is commonly said, is the paradise of quacks. Whoever sufficiently advertises the most worthless nostrum becomes rich; whoever preaches a faith-cure, or a science cure, or a magnetic cure, or a blue-glass cure, finds a crowd of fools for followers. In the presence of the evils caused by this universal quackery, should the physician confine himself simply to the treatment of disease? Is it not his duty as a lover of God and of man, as a patriot and a scholar, whether he lives in some isolated hamlet or in a great city, to become a public teacher? Who else is able to diffuse the knowledge of the laws of health and the causes of disease with so much authority and ability? To those who should object that the popularizing of medical science might prove hurtful, I would reply that belief in the good of ignorance or the harmfulness of knowledge is superstition. It is always good to know a thing, and the evils which the spread of intelligence may cause are not only more than counterbalanced by the benefits knowledge confers, but they tend to correct themselves. If ignorance is bliss, it is the bliss of fools or cowards. When an epidemic threatens there is a general alarm and every precaution is taken to exclude it; but the foes of life are always around us, lying in ambush. They may lurk in the air we breathe, in the food we eat, in the water we drink, in the clothing we wear, in the houses we live in, in the domestic animals that supply us with nourishment or lie about our hearths, on the lips of those we love. It is believed that we all are intelligent enough when our interests are at stake, but professional men know how false is this tenet. It is a delusion to imagine that the multitude think. Their notions of health, of right, of religion, are traditional or empirical, and to rouse them to self-activity, to observation, and reflection, is the best work an enlightened mind can perform. "As a man thinketh in his heart, so is he." "With desolation is the earth made desolate, because there is no one who thinketh within his heart." To take but a partial view of the subject, does not daily experience teach the physician, the lawyer and the priest, that the ignorance, the thoughtlessness and indifference of those who seek their help are chief impediments to the success of their efforts to render service? Those who know least, not only misunderstand us, but they are also quickest to condemn. In diffusing knowledge we, of the learned professions, work for our own good not less than for the general welfare. The more intelligent the people are, the more responsive they become to the teachings of religion and science. Sanitary regulations enable civilized nations to exclude or control pestilence and contagion. A proper system of sewerage seems to have freed Memphis from the epidemics which threatened its existence. There is not a farm-house, not a cottage in the smallest village, in which a knowledge of the laws of health and of the causes of disease might not be made the means of saving human lives. How seldom are the heads of families practically attentive to the fact that water may be limpid and pleasant to the taste and yet carry the germs of fatal maladies, which may lurk even, with merely suspended vitality, in the clearest ice! How little do they heed the seeds of disease which are concealed in damp cellars, in unventilated rooms, in unaired closets, in carpets, in the cushions of chairs, and in the dried sputa of the tuberculous! The land is filled with the clamorous denouncers of drunkenness and poisonous liquors; but gluttony and badly prepared food are the causes of more sickness and misery than alcoholic drink, and the army of reformers might well reserve part of the abuse they heap upon distillers and saloon-keepers for cooks and confectioners. My argument against women is that they have made us a nation of dyspeptics, having from time immemorial held undisputed sway in the kitchen. Why should we entrust the framing of our laws to those who have ruined our stomachs? If the food they eat were less indigestible men would be more sober. How few practically recognize the fact that the function the skin performs is as essential to health as that of the lungs, or the liver, or the kidneys! Is it not strange that the daily bath should not have been made a prescription of religion, since cleanliness is next to godliness? At all events it is a secret of health and long life, and he is a wise physician who makes himself an advocate of frequent ablutions. How is it possible to like or even respect those who fail to begin each day by plunging in the purifying wave, or, at least, by showering over themselves the clear and silvery spray. I should, without much hesitation, give my confidence to a stranger about whom I might know little else than that he never omits this clean ablution whether the thermometer register thirty degrees below or ninety degrees above zero; but with one who does not bathe I should not care to have any dealings. When I reflect how unwashed many of the heroes must have been, from Hector to Bonaparte, with the itch, I feel a sense of disillusion; and when I hear Americans praised, what pleases me most is the assertion that they bathe more than other people. The bath is not merely hygienic; it is a test of civilization.

Who, so well as the physician, is able to impart a knowledge of the laws of heredity in their bearing upon disease and immorality? Why should foolish young people be permitted to marry, when every wise man knows that their union will result in a diseased or depraved offspring? The end of marriage is not to console weak and sentimental beings, but to provide a nobler race. As the life of the soul is enrooted in that of the body, the physician is called to minister to moral as well as to physical infirmities. An American doctor, as you know, claims to have discovered a cure for drunkenness; and whether or not his remedies have any efficacy, it is a gain to create a wide recognition of the fact that dipsomania, in many cases, at least, is a disease of the nervous system. Indeed, it seems to be altogether probable, that sensual excess of whatever kind is as often the result as the cause of abnormal physical conditions. If this be so, what a world is not opened to the medical profession wherein they may labor with the hope of being able to confer on their fellow-men not bodily health alone, but moral and religious blessings as well?

Whoever belongs to a learned profession should have more than professional knowledge and skill. He should be a representative of the science and the culture of his age. Where the standard of education for the liberal professions is low, the life of the nation cannot be high.

Human perfection is health of body and soul, manifesting itself in the wholesome activity of every function and faculty; and in a free country the natural stimulators of this activity are the lawyer, the physician, and the minister of religion. In a democracy, if the people are to escape the rule of demagogues and thieves, they must have the guidance of superior minds and great characters, and where shall they be found if not in the liberal professions? As I look upon the professions, they are all religious, for the end and aim of all of them is to make health, justice, and righteousness prevail; and what is this but to make the will of God prevail?

Nor has the physician a baser office than the lawyer or the priest. If you cripple the animal in man, you clip the angel's wings, for the nobler passions draw their life and energy from the lower. Many things, we might imagine, are dearer than life,— honor, for instance, and truth and love; but in all this, as in whatever else has worth, life is present and gives it value. What we first demand of professional men whatever their special calling, is that they be upright, honorable and humane. Character is essential, for character gives to ability its human quality, makes it something we can trust, makes it beneficent. Thus I complete my earlier thought that professional men are united by indissoluble bonds. They all alike find their reason for being, in the needs and miseries of man; they all minister to his ills, and to all, science, culture, and religion supply the means which render them able to help.

A classic writer has said that no better fortune can befall a city than to have within its walls two or three superior men who agree to work together for the common welfare. Who shall these two or three superior men be, if not the lawyer, the physician, and the minister of religion? They are found in every village, and if they hold themselves abreast of the science and culture of the age, and are also men of character, who shall estimate the value of their combined influence? It is the nature of science, culture, and religion to be communicable, and they who diffuse these blessings are the most useful and the noblest men. They alone have the right to say to their fellows: Provide for us, while we make your lives more healthful and pleasant, purer and higher.

But how shall I, a Kentuckian, addressing, for the first time in many years, an audience of Kentuckians, close without growing conscious of the inspiration of my native air? So long as we can recall with pleasure the divine moments of our youth, they have not wholly fled, but when they come back to us like mocking questioners, asking what good or truth or beauty there was in the things which once filled us with delight, then alas! youth is gone, forever gone, and we have ceased to be ourselves. But oh! I can remember, how in the days of my young love, walking in the fields and in the woods that lay about my home, I scarcely knew my feet touched the ground, but felt that my deep glowing soul might mount heavenward until it blended with the infinite ether, and became immortal harmonious pulsings of light and warmth, of joy and ecstasy. And later, how often from the Cincinnati hills have I looked southward across the river and seemed to behold there a fairer world,— looked with a longing such as Adam may have felt when he turned his eyes towards lost paradise.

> Not Syracuse, nor the fair Grecian plain
>  Saw coursers swift as thine, sweet home of mine,
>  Nor did their sacrificial herds outshine
> Thine own, whose silken flanks are without stain.
>
> Not there on rarer flowers fell warm, spring rain,
>  Nor wore the heavens a beauty more divine,
>  Nor purer maidens knelt at holy shrine,
> Nor braver men held warlike death for gain.

> Thou wantest but the poet to waft thy name
>   In rhythmic numbers through the earth and sky,
> Some bard divine, with strong, heroic aim,
>   To soar aloft, and utter deathless cry;
> No muse has touched thy lips with sacred flame,
>   To bid the music flow which cannot die.

Our country is greater than our State; it fills us with larger and nobler thoughts, rouses the consciousness of a mightier and more far-reaching destiny. It is worthy of all homage and love for what it has done, and more worthy still for what it promises to do. In the presence of its boundless energies, aspirations, and sympathies, the greatest even feel they are dwarfed. But our country, in a more intimate sense, is our home. He who has no home has no country. Patriotism is the spirit of the father's house, which is the home of our first love and the one to which we turn our last lingering thoughts as death's curtain drops. Hence our State comes closer to us than our country; it awakens tenderer recollections, weaves about us the tendrils of more gentle and fragrant affections. It calls forth feelings which glow like the dawn, which soften and mellow like the evening sky. It blends with memories of the twining arms of mothers and fathers, of the warm, unselfish devotion of youthful friends. The thought of it is interfused with clouds and showers and the songs of birds, and all the glories of the unfolding world that accompanied us when we were young.

State rights in the old sense are dead, but while the heart of a Kentuckian throbs State pride cannot die. How shall we better serve our country than by loving our State and doing what in us lies to strengthen, purify, and illumine the life of its citizens? I ask these learned physicians whether a climate which produces the noblest breeds of animals, should not be favorable to the noblest breed of men?

What does our country or our State, what does God himself demand of us, but that we grow to the full measure of the gifts we have received?

We render the best service when we make ourselves worthy and wise. The faithful servant of any cause is not a vulgar boaster, but a true striver after the best things.

When Jenner consulted Dr. Hunter as to whether he might not substitute vaccination for inoculation, he received the reply: "Don't think, but try." He tried and was successful. The right motto, however, is this: "Think and try, try and think." Only God can set limits to what thought and effort may accomplish.

I will not exhort, for that would be to reproach, I will not proffer advice, for that would be to insult, but I will ask whether you know anything better than the pursuit of excellence? Equality is a figment of theorists, inequality is nature's law. As well not be at all as be common. If the equality at which democracy aims means the ostracism of superior men, it is a curse; a blessing, if it means the placing of superior men in the lead that they may guide the whole people to nobler ideals and higher truth. The best freedom is that which is favorable to the development of high and heroic personalities; the best education that which fills us with desire for all that is excellent. It is good to be wise and virtuous, but it is also good to be healthy, strong, brave, honorable, fair, and graceful. It is bad to be ignorant and sinful, but it is also bad to be sick, weak, cowardly, base, ugly, and awkward. The striving after perfection, in this large sense, blesses and dignifies life. It is a cure for many ills; it makes us independent, sufficient for ourselves, able to forego praise and patronage; for if men seek not our aid, when we have made ourselves worthy and capable, the loss is theirs, not ours. In pursuing these high aims, we feel that we are living for God and our country, and we may even deem ourselves fortunate that in the early years of our professional career we have little else to do than to improve ourselves. Happy is he who having found the highest thing he is able to do, gives his life to the work.

Go forth, then, young gentlemen, to perform

the noble and humane tasks that will be set you. The dawn of a more glorious day has risen upon your profession. With Hutten you may exclaim: " O blessed age ! Minds awaken, sciences bloom, — it is a joy to be alive." To every home you visit you shall bring promise of life and health, and it will not be your fault, if when you depart, you leave not a sense of security and peace. So live, that when in the future there shall be speech of the worthiest Kentuckians, of you also mention shall be made.

# CHAPTER V.

### THEORIES OF LIFE AND EDUCATION.

*That one should be ignorant who has capacity for knowledge,—this I call tragedy.* CARLYLE.

TO write a perfect logic, it would be necessary to write a perfect treatise on man; and a complete theory of education would be a complete philosophy of human nature. The aim and end of education is to bring out and strengthen man's faculties, physical, intellectual, and moral; to call into healthful play his manifold capacities; and to promote also with due subordination their harmonious exercise; and thus to fit him to fulfil his high and heaven-given mission, and to attain his true destiny. This would seem to be simple enough, and the most opposite schools of thought would probably find this statement sufficiently large to embrace all their differences. Nevertheless the subject of education is among the most involved and difficult, as it is among those which bear most directly upon the highest and holiest interests of mankind. The difficulty comes in part from the nature of man, which is complex. By thought he belongs to the world of intellect; by will to the moral world: his body makes him brother to the sluggish clod; his soul gives him companionship with angels, and the whole circumstance of his existence involves him in the most complicated relations with his fellow-beings. There is not merely diversity in his endowments, but contrariety.

The difficulty increases when we come to consider the modifications produced by his surroundings, — the ever-varying and counteracting influences which affect his character; and yet, in such manner that to assign to each cause its proper effect in the total result is impossible. Again, the phases of human nature in the same individual are so various; the types of collective bodies of men, so dissimilar; the features of the different national characters, so unlike; the effects produced by the same cause upon the same person, at different times, so opposite; the force of climate, of physical constitution, and even of the most trivial accidental circumstances, so marked, and yet so little subject to human foresight, — that, taken collectively, these facts of themselves seem to show, that the question of man's perfect and complete education is most intricate and involved. No one has a clear knowledge of the history even of his own life; of the causes of his progress and retrogression; of the influences that surrounded the birth of his affections and the cradle of his thoughts; of the motives that impelled him in this direction or in that. Were it possible to see ourselves as we are, it would yet be impossible to see clearly the causes which have made us what we are. Religious faith; the circumstances of birth and country; the national institutions and literature; the scenes and occupations of childhood; habits, whether good or evil, formed in youth; these and a thousand other influences, often obscure and difficult to trace, go to mould a human character.

There are persons who have been confirmed in virtue by having the bitterness of sin and the folly of wrong-doing brought home to them by sad experience. Others, on the contrary, having once gone astray, never return to the right path, but wander and ever wander, as though, like our first parents, by a first fall, their very nature had been tainted. Who can determine the influence of temperament and of inherited disposition in any given character? And yet this influence ought to be kept in view by the educator. There are natures which are strengthened and ennobled by a discipline which would weaken and degrade those whose endowments are of a different kind. What fine discernment and deep insight are needed to bring out the antagonistic faculties without permitting them to clash and mutilate one another. The mechanical trade which requires the use of the arms alone, gives to them an abnormal strength at the expense of other members of the body, and thus destroys the symmetry and beauty of the human frame. Excess of physical exercise diminishes the power to think; and great devotion to intellectual culture has a tendency, not only to weaken the body, but to enfeeble the strength of moral conviction also, and consequently to undermine the basis of all true character. The pure intellect is not the sufficient measure of the reality of things, and overweening confidence in its power leads to scepticism. In the same way the development of the will and of moral consciousness, without corresponding mental enlightenment, may beget superstition and fanaticism, — "the zeal which is not of knowledge." Even in the same faculty there is such a diversity of operation, that the education of the intellect or of the conscience alone, if we could consider them as isolated, would still be most difficult. Imagination is developed at the expense of judgment; the power of analysis interferes with the more wholesome synthetic operations of the mind;

and metaphysical intuition is often found in inverse ratio to common sense. Equilibrium of moral character is not more easily produced. Considered in themselves, the virtues all conspire to form the perfect man; but the limitations of human nature prevent this ideal harmony; and hence, we find that courage interferes with meekness, independence with humility, generosity with economy, and confidence with prudence. The difficulty then is manifest, and it is also evident that no system can be devised by which a perfect education will be secured. And, in fact, to trust greatly to any educational mechanism is a dangerous illusion. Growth of soul is a spiritual process, and can be promoted only by spiritual agencies. Man, and not the school system, is the true educator; and to believe that machinery, so powerful within its own sphere, is also able to form worthy men and women, is a gross superstition. It is none the less true, however, that education cannot be carried on without the aid of mechanical appliances; and hence the necessity of systems, and of attempts to realize them. Every system of education is based upon a theory, which is derived from views concerning man's nature and destiny. What is man? What ought he to be? What is his chief business in life? Has he a destiny beyond this life? If so, has his conduct in this life a bearing upon his future state? These are questions which necessarily come up for consideration when we attempt to form a theory of education; and this theory will be shaped by the answers which we accept. A system of education is, in fact, the expression of a universal philosophy, embracing God, man, and nature; and hence, nothing throws more light upon the real thought of an age than its views upon this subject. An attentive examination of this matter will not only reveal what men really hold to be true, but it will also bring out, as in relief, the relative importance which they attach to their professed beliefs, and the strength of conviction with which they hold them.

In illustration, we will first revert to the classic nations, whose religion was a kind of nature-worship, and who, though they believed in a future existence, looked upon this life as alone joyous and happy. Hellenic religion, which had its origin in the deification of nature, found its highest expression in the state, whose tutelary divinities were the heroes by whom it had been founded or successfully defended. The state was absolute and supreme; and man's first duty and privilege was to be of service to his country. The future life was to be cheerless in the land of shadows and gloom; here we drink in the blessed light and air of heaven; here is the green earth, here the flowing waters, here all things invite to joy.

In accordance with these views of man and life, education among the Greeks is patriotic and æsthetic. In Sparta, the sole aim is to discipline the man into the perfect soldier, and at Athens an element of culture and refinement is added, which is opposed to the warlike temper, and the influence of which led to the decay of Grecian civilization. The moral education which teaches the individual that he has duties and responsibilities which transcend his earthly sphere, and which make him accountable to an infinite Being, and an order of things which is eternal, was neglected. In his noblest work Plato has left us an elaborate theory of education, in which he sacrifices both the freedom of the individual and the rights of the family to the state.

With the Romans, too, the state was supreme; but their character was more serious and practical than that of the cheerful and pleasure-loving Greeks. And hence, to the military training which prepared them to win victories for their country, was added a juristic education which taught them to watch jealously over their rights. When by the conquest of

Greece, they were brought into contact with æsthetic culture, it was again found incompatible with the patriotic and military temper, and gradually undermined Roman as it had destroyed Grecian civilization. Religion was held to be a function of the state, and hence religious education was made subordinate and auxiliary to the patriotic spirit. Man's first and highest duty was to his country; and both the individual and the family were sacrificed to the state. Hellenism is negatively characterized by want of moral earnestness. The Greek is intellectually active; is eager to see things as they are, and finds the most childlike and real delight in whatever is beautiful; but he has no sense of sin, no awful consciousness of God's presence and holiness. He argues and disputes; creates philosophy and poetry and all the arts, but perishes for having failed to perceive the paramount importance of conduct. His desire to see things as they are, degenerates into sophistry; his love of the beautiful becomes sensuality; and he himself remains an eternal example of the impotence of the noblest endowments, where there is no basis of moral earnestness and religious faith.

Judaism took a different view of man, and consequently formed a different theory of education. The idea of God, the Creator of all things, and wholly free from the control of nature, is the dominant thought of Hebraism. Hence man's primal duty is not to deified personifications of natural forces, but to God, who loves righteousness and hates iniquity; whose will is law, and its fulfilment blessedness; and its violation, which is sin, the only evil and supreme misery. Nature is no longer independent and self-existent, as in the Greek's conception, but a creature, and hence the Hebrew is freed from her control, and loves and fears God alone. Far from adoring as divine the beauty revealed in nature, he flees from it as a temptation to idolatry. For a similar reason, the state cannot be absolute and supreme, and prominence is given to the family. Education is patriarchal and religious, and is directed chiefly to morality.

To illustrate still further the manner in which the theory of education conforms to the generally accepted ideal of man, let us turn from the consideration of national types to the class type.

In the Middle Ages, the most characteristic figures are the knight and the monk. The ideal of chivalry is free military service in behalf of Christendom, and consequently in behalf of all who are wronged and oppressed; and among these, woman takes precedence by virtue of the supreme charm with which she appeals to the heart of man. With a view to fit him for this noble career, the boy, when he was seven years old, began to learn the manner of offensive and defensive warfare, on foot and on horseback; and between his sixteenth and eighteenth year he was raised to knighthood by a formal ceremony. His intellectual education was neglected, as having nothing to do with the main purpose of his life. His hand was to hold the sword and not the pen; and even in modern times we find, in proportion as the aristocratic spirit is powerful, a want of mental flexibility and openness to ideas in the nobility. Great development was given to the moral qualities which go to form the knightly character, especially courage and the sense of honor. To be a true knight, was to be *sans peur et sans reproche.* The exaggerated notion of the worth of courage and the extreme sensibility to honor, which were fostered by this education, led to the fantastic extravagancy of knight-errantry, and finally degenerated into vagabondism and quixotism, which were the harbingers of the decline and dissolution of chivalry.

Education is the effort to create the ideal man, whether absolutely or relatively to special vocations, and hence the theory will conform to the received notions concerning this ideal. When the first requisite of a perfect man is thought to be a strong and athletic body, gymnastic exercise will take precedence of intellectual training; when the chief good is held to be an enlightened mind, mental activity will be stimulated, even though the body should suffer. Again, each vocation will have its special education. The training of the soldier will be different from that of the lawyer; the physician will not be educated like the priest. A fashionable mother, who thinks woman's vocation is to please and to be pleased, will send her daughter to a school of manners, where she will be taught the graces and accomplishments of artificial and frivolous society. The unlikeness of the different special educations arises from the dissimilar ideals of the various vocations. Knowledge, whether got in a military academy or a commercial college, is equally good, but knowledge is not education. Habits of thought and of life are more than knowledge, and the habits which are necessarily acquired during the process of education may render knowledge useless or hurtful. Every educated man knows much that may be to his advantage in any position, but in getting this knowledge he has probably formed habits which, in avocations different from the one for which he has been trained, will be of greater injury than his learning will be of help. And hence Roger Bacon's axiom, that "knowledge is power," is fallacious. The soldier has doubtless learned many things which the tradesman ought to know, but he has also conceived a notion of life, of honor, of the value of courage, as compared with other qualities, which, were he forced to become a merchant, would prove to be obstacles to his success.

"An Oxford education," says Mr. Froude, "fits a man extremely well for the trade of gentleman. I do not know for what other trade it does fit him as at present constituted. More than one man who has taken high honors there, who has learnt faithfully all that the university undertakes to teach him, has been seen in these late years breaking stones upon a road in Australia." A better stone-breaker he would doubtless have been had he never studied at Oxford.

An illustration of the truth upon which I am here insisting is furnished by American society. A scientific education gives to the farmer knowledge which he can put to practical use in a thousand ways. Chemistry, zoölogy, botany, physiology, mineralogy, and physics generally, may in his hands be converted into money. Shall we not, then, give to every farmer a scientific education? No; for the habits of thought and sentiment which such education creates would render farm life distasteful to him; and in fact, we find in our own country that even a little education tends to drive the young men from tillage of the land to the shop life of towns and cities, or, worse still, into the learned professions, and our agricultural colleges train young men for everything except the work for which they were organized.

It can hardly be necessary to insist further upon the essential relation which exists between the theory of human destiny and the theory of human education. The question, what education shall I give my child? can be answered only by asking another question, What do you desire your child to be and to do? The accepted end of man determines the aim of the educator and prescribes his system. Now there are two radically different ways of viewing human life, and but two. We may consider it as complete in this world, or as preparatory to a higher state of existence, and corresponding to these opposite views we have the secular and the religious theories of education. If there is no future life, a system of education based upon the recognition of such life must be false and hurtful. The human mind in matters of this kind refuses to accept arguments drawn from expediency. To hold that there is no God and no immortal human soul, and yet to educate men to believe in God and in the soul from a notion that such teaching has a social value, is an outrage. Rather let the race perish than be kept alive by an infinite lie and worldwide imposture. On the other hand, to hold that God is, and that the soul is immortal, and yet to refuse to make the system of education conformable to this belief, is an outrage; and here again the human mind refuses to accept arguments drawn from expedience. Whether or not this kind of education will best serve the cause of what is called civilization and progress, is of small moment. If God is, He is first, He is all in all; if the soul is, it is more than civilization and progress.

These two opposite views of human life are in fatal antagonism, and there can be no thought of compromise; they give form and character to the two hostile armies in the eternal warfare between spirit and matter, the temporal and the eternal, the Christ and the world. That the view whose horizon is bounded by man's present life is widely accepted, there can be no doubt. It has its philosophy, its ethics, its political economy, its sociology, its pedagogy, and hopes to have its religion. It is not a happy or joyful belief, yet it is full of confidence and eager courage, — a confidence and a courage born not of an accidental or a casual insight into the nature of things, but of a range of thought which embraces the universe, which weighs the atom and the sun, which meditates devoutly upon the life of the animalcule and seeks to trace it in uninterrupted ascent to man, which studies with a courage that never despairs the most hidden nerve-force, hoping against hope that it will yet detect it breaking into thought and soul life. It has not the mocking and frivolous temper of Voltaire, nor the satanic mood of Byron. So wide has its thought grown, that fanaticism is almost impossible. As Schiller grieved over the dead gods of Greece, this new philosophy is filled with the quiet sorrow of fatalism in contemplating the old faith. There is a kind of exultation as the light breaks in upon the hidden mysteries of nature, but in every cry of triumph there is an undertone of sadness, almost of despair, as from a half-conscious feeling that the end of all is death and darkness and nothingness, so that what began as the most self-satisfied optimism, now fatally turns to pessimism, which is the protest of the unbelieving soul against sensualism and atheism.

Let us trace the theoretical development of this earth-creed, and then study its historical manifestation, in so far as it bears upon the question of education and man's destiny. I shall not go further back than Kant, who is the father of the critical philosophy, and who gave the impulse to the intellectual movement, which, outside the Church, is bearing the modern mind farther and farther away from metaphysics. It was he who first inspired a profound distrust of whatever is beyond the sphere of experience; and who relegated to the region of the unknown the reality which underlies the phenomenon. The result of his thinkings is this: The phenomenon alone can be known; the noumenon is not cognoscible.

The human reason is involved in radical contradictions whenever it attempts to dogmatize concerning God, the soul, and the universe; and hence arise, by a necessary process, the paralogisms of theology, the gratuitous hypotheses of psychology and the antinomies of cosmology. Here we have the essential principles of the Positivism of Comte, and of the Cosmism of Herbert Spencer, — absolute condemnation of metaphysics, scepticism concerning the operations of our highest faculties, and the elimination of all reality which is not perceived by the senses.

The influence of Hegel, which has been so profoundly felt by the modern world, is in the same direction. The identity of being and not being; the personality of God, an absurdity unworthy of the attention of serious thinkers; the efficient and final cause of the world immanent in the world; nothing is, but everything is becoming; truth and reality consequently nothing absolute, but fugitive forms of what neither is, nor is not, — a kind of intellectual star-dust, which is not nothing nor anything. These are some of the characteristic doctrines of Hegelian pantheism, and whatever else may be thought of them, they unmistakably confine the life of man to this world, which is its own efficient and final cause. The universe is an eternal flow, in which truth and beauty and goodness are but the changeful waves that float upon the great world-current of matter. Each fact, each individual, is a point of momentary rest in the midst of universal mobility.

In this system religion has but an accidental value, and the interest which it inspires is chiefly historical and psychological. The forms in which man has clothed his dreams of the divine are curious as an archæological study or as a branch of ethnology. The vulgar and passionate polemics of Protestantism and rationalism are obsolete. Nothing is false or in bad taste, but dogmatism. Christianity is man's highest effort to give form and body to the infinite, and when criticism shall have finally done away with all its dogmas, it will be left to the inspirations of the heart, to be transformed indefinitely to suit the requirements of progress and civilization. There is no God, but there are divine things, — culture, liberty and love. This is the soil in which the religion of humanity flourishes; the worship of man taking the place of the worship of God. In the beginning there is no God, there is nothing, only a becoming; in the end, there is man. He is the highest, let us serve him. And since the individual is but a bubble that bursts and remerges in the general air, a snowflake, remelting into the element from which it was assumed and congealed into separateness, let him dwindle and let the race be more and more. Let the weak perish, let the fittest survive, let all things belong to the strong. This is the eternal law of our sacred mother, Nature, who alone is supreme. An ideal humanity, truly, is only an abstraction; it does not exist, it will never exist; it is but a phantom. The individual is contemptible. The race is found only in the individual. All this is undeniable. But what will you have? Our hypothesis excludes God, and this phantom of humanity is all that remains to persuade us that to eat and to drink is not the only wisdom. In this system too, the religion of pantheistic mysticism, the faith of Carlyle and of Emerson, finds its justification. Pantheism is obscure and nebular, and mysticism loves the uncertain light of a symbolical and oracular phraseology, and when the two are combined, it is not easy to seize the real thought. The thought, however, is pantheistic, the mood is mystic. The central idea, upon which the thousand changes of poetic and prophetic rhapsody are rung, and from which also proceed objurgation, scorn, anger, indignation, withering contempt, whether in the jolting, interrupted, epigrammatic style of Emerson, or in the tumultuous, turgid, apodictic manner of Carlyle, is Pantheism. For both the efficient and final cause of the world is immanent in the world, and the transcendentalism is modal and accidental. To both, systems and creeds are hateful, and to be "a swallower of formulas" is the highest glory. As there is no absolute truth, there is no permanent symbol. To be spontaneous, original, and strong, is the only merit. The world's great men know no other law than the fatality of their genius. To be weak is, as Milton says, the true misery.

"Thus," says Carlyle, "like some wild-flaming, wild-thundering train of Heaven's artillery, does this mysterious MANKIND thunder and flame in long-drawn, quick-succeeding grandeur through the unknown deep. Thus like a God-created, fire-breathing spirit-host, we emerge from the inane, haste stormfully across the astonished earth, then plunge again into the inane." A rushing forth from nothing back into nothing, — this is all. The educator's business is to prepare man to make this stormful haste across the astonished earth in a becoming manner.

Pedagogy cannot aspire to fit him for an existence in the inane. For this life must man be educated; of another, if other there is, neither knowledge nor faith can give us true account. The hero of Carlyle's profoundest and most eloquent work, walks wearisomely through this world, having lost all tidings of another and higher. Fixed, starless, tartarean darkness envelops his soul. "The everlasting NO had said: 'Behold, thou art fatherless, outcast, and the universe is mine.'" The hero made answer: "I am not thine, but free, and forever hate thee." This wild protest against despair leads him to the Centre of

Indifference, from which in grim mockery he hurls his objurgations: "God," he says, "must needs laugh outright, could such a thing be, to see his wondrous manikins here below." He is in the wilderness; it is the wide world in an atheistic century.

Lying here in this Centre of Indifference he awakes to a new heaven and a new earth. From a high table-land he gazes upon the world and contemplates its myriadfold and ever-changing forms of beauty and life. "How thou fermentest," he exclaims, "and elaboratest in thy great fermenting vat and laboratory of an atmosphere, of a world! Oh, nature! or, what is nature? Ha! Why do I not name thee God? Art not thou the 'living garment of God?' Oh, Heavens, is it, in very deed, He, then, that ever speaks through thee; that lives and loves in thee, that lives and loves in me?"

And to this pantheism the spirit of mysticism comes to seek a new worship. The Mythus of Christianity is obsolete. "The temple thereof, founded some eighteen centuries ago, now lies in ruins, overgrown with jungle, the habitation of doleful creatures." A worship and an ideal nevertheless must be found. Speculation is by nature endless, formless, a vortex amid vortices. Thought fatally leads to the abyss in which all things whirl in inextricable confusion, and in which nothing can be seen or known with certainty; for in the lowest deep a lower depth still opening swallows the thinker and his thought, beyond plummet's sounding, yea, beyond the reach of fantasy. The end of life, therefore, is not to think, but to act. Not that we might in morbid self-introspection eat our own hearts; projecting upon the world we rail at our diseased imaginations, have we emerged from the inane. Goethe is right. His immortal precept opens a new era and founds a new religion. Study, he says, how to live; that is, study how to make the most of life. "Fool! the ideal is in thyself, the impediment too is in thyself; thy condition is but the stuff thou art to shape that same ideal out of; what matters whether such stuff be of this sort or that, so the form thou give it be heroic, be poetic? O thou that pinest in the imprisonment of the actual, and criest bitterly to the gods for a kingdom wherein to rule and create, know this of a truth. The thing thou seekest is already with thee, 'here or nowhere,' couldst thou only see." Here or nowhere, study how to make the most of life. This is the path that leads upward from tartarean darkness and endless chaos to the light and serenity of cosmic harmony. Carlyle, most assuredly, is no materialist, he is no utilitarian; and just as little is he a sensualist or a scientific atheist. Against all these things his soul cries out in fiery and convulsive indignation. What an imperishable odor is there not in those "pig propositions" in which he gives us the materialist and utilitarian theory of the world? The universe is an immeasurable swine's trough. Moral evil is unattainability of pig's wash. Paradise, called also state of innocence, age of gold, was unlimited attainability of pig's wash. It is the mission of universal pighood, and the duty of all pigs, at all times, to diminish the quantity of unattainable, and increase that of attainable. All knowledge and device and effort ought to be directed thither, and thither only. Pig poetry ought to consist of universal recognition of the excellence of pig's wash and ground barley, and the felicity of pigs whose trough is in order, and who have had enough. Humph! Who made the pig? Unknown; perhaps the pork butcher.

The cold and pitiless irony of Swift is here seething hot, like molten lava.

Scientific atheism, too, with its superficial and self-conceited rationalism, fills him with contempt, in which there is also an element of fiery anger. "Thou wilt have no mystery and mysticism, he exclaims; wilt walk through thy world by the sunshine of what thou callest truth, or even by the hand-lamp of what I call attorney-logic, and 'explain' all, 'account' for all, or believe nothing of it. Nay, thou wilt attempt laughter; whoso recognizes the unfathomable, all-pervading domain of mystery, which is everywhere, under our feet and among our hands; to whom the universe is an oracle and temple, as well as a kitchen and cattle-stall, — he shall be a delirious mystic; to him, thou, with sniffing charity, wilt protrusively proffer thy hand-lamp, and shriek as one injured when he kicks his foot through it." The universe is awful, mysterious. "Thy daily life is girt with wonder, and based on wonder; thy very blankets and breeches are miracles." The unspeakable divine significance lies in all things. "Atheistic science babbles poorly of it, with scientific nomenclatures, experiments, and what not, as if it were a poor dead thing to be bottled up in Leyden jars and sold over counters. But the natural sense of man, in all times, if he will honestly apply his sense, knows it to be a living thing, — ah, an unspeakable, Godlike thing, towards which the best attitude for us after never so much science, is awe, devout prostration and humility of soul; worship, if not in words, then in silence." This indignant rebuke to atheism proceeds from a fervent soul. Impiety is offensive to Carlyle, to whom whatever is, is divine, is God. All religions he holds are good, if only men are sincere. The only idolatry is that from which the sentiment has departed. To worship sticks and stones with all one's heart and in downright honesty, is better than all the conventional pieties of our modern world. The value of religion is purely subjective; it is in the sentiment. The object is of small moment, for all possible symbols are but representations of the mysterious unknown which lies beneath appearance. But for Carlyle, as for all who deny the existence of a personal God, man is the highest; and his religion is hero-worship. His view is fixed upon this life alone; he knows no other. Here or nowhere. Man rushes forth from nothing back into nothing. To educate him for a future life, would be as absurd as to educate him for a past life. In fact, as he had no past life, so will he have no future life. Study, therefore, to make the most of this; and to teach this highest and only wisdom, should be the educator's aim and purpose. Carlyle, however, has no faith in any mechanism or system of education. A gerund-grinding pedagogue is to him no better than the wood and leather man whom the Nurembergers were to build, and "who should reason as well as most country parsons." The curse of the age is its belief in mechanism. The soul of man, the soul of society, the soul of religion, is come to be considered the product of mechanical action. If the wheels, cogs, valves, pistons, and checks are in order, all is well. Man's happiness and worth are no longer believed to be within himself; his ideal is not a spiritual and divine something, but an outward condition, in which there will be well-oiled and smoothly working machines for manufacturing everything; from patent creeds and codes to patent breeches. This is atheism, this is infinite evil, infinite despair, and no-religion. "We have forgotten God," he says, "in the most modern dialect and very pith of the matter, we have taken up the fact of this universe as it *is not*. We have quietly closed our eyes to the eternal substance of things, and opened them only to the shows and shams of things. We quietly believe the universe to be intrinsically a great unintelligible PERHAPS; extrinsically clear enough it is a great, most extensive cattlefold and workhouse, with most extensive kitchen ranges, dining tables, — whereat he is wise who can find a place! All the truth of this universe is uncertain; only the profit and loss of it, the pudding and praise of it, are and remain very visible to the practical man. There is no God any longer for us! God's laws are become a greatest happiness principle, a parliamentary expediency; the heavens overarch us only as an astronomical timekeeper. . . . This is verily the plague-spot centre of the universal social gangrene, threatening all modern things with frightful death. To him that will consider it, here is the stem, with its roots and tap-root, with its world-wide upas-boughs and accursed poison exudations, under which the world lies writhing in atrophy and agony. You touch the fatal centre of all our disease, of our frightful nosology of diseases, when you lay your hand on this." "There is no religion; there is no God; man has lost his soul, and vainly seeks antiseptic salt." The blight of this faith in what is dead, godless, and mechanic, corrupts our modern education, which regards only what is practical and economic, and wholly abandons to moral dry-rot man's spiritual and religious nature. The science of the age is physical, chemical, physiological. Even mathematics is valued only for its mechanic use, in building bridges, constructing forts, and indicating the proper angle for killing men at given distances. The inventor of the spinning-jenny and sewing-machine has his reward. The philosopher is without honor. Thought is secreted by the brain; and poetry and religion are "a product of the smaller intestines." What other than a mechanical education is possible to men who breathe this mephitic, soul-stifling air? The mind is littered, as though it grew like a vegetable, with etymological and other compost; it is crammed with dead vocables; it is taught that its chief use is to calculate profit and loss; and when it is burnt out to a grammatical and arithmetical cinder, its education is complete.

"Alas, so is it everywhere, so will it ever be; till the hodman is discharged or reduced to hod-bearing and an architect is hired, and on all hands fitly encouraged; till communities and individuals discover, not without surprise, that fashioning the souls of a generation by knowledge, can rank on a level with blowing their bodies to pieces by gunpowder; that with generals and field-marshals, for killing, there should be world-honored dignitaries, and were it possible, true God-ordained priests for teaching."

No hidebound pedant can educate. Of man, such a one knows only that he has a faculty called memory, and that it can be acted on through the muscular integument by birchen rods. To educate we must touch the mysterious springs of love, fear, and wonder, of enthusiasm, poetry, religion. These are the inward and vital powers of man; who cannot be roused into deep, all-pervading effort by any computable prospect of profit and loss, for any definite finite object, but only for what is invisible and infinite. "When we can drain the ocean into our mill-ponds, and bottle up the force of gravity, to be sold by retail in our gas-jars, then we may hope to comprehend the infinitudes of man's soul under formulas of profit and loss; and rule over this too, as over a patent engine, by checks and valves and balances."

One of Carlyle's great merits is the vividness and force with which he brings out man's spiritual nature; his craving for the infinite; his inborn and necessary dissatisfaction with whatever is not eternal and all-perfect. Out of the meanness and littleness and emptiness of the world which surrounds him, he takes refuge in the eternities, the immensities, the veracities. It is at least singular that the most gifted and earnest writers of the England of the nineteenth century, in spite of their innumerable differences in thought and temper, should agree in their estimate of English life. That it is low and vulgar, selfish and insincere, without high ideals or generous impulses or noble aspirations, is the common testimony of Carlyle and John Stuart Mill, of Dickens and Thackeray, of Byron and Tennyson, of Ruskin and Matthew Arnold. Macaulay, indeed, is inclined to optimistic views in whatever concerns England, but he is purely literary; lives on the surface, which he rounds off with a polished and ornate phrase, and leaves untouched the deep central heart of things.

What gloomy energy is there not in the following words of Carlyle! —

"Like the valley of Jehoshaphat it lies round us, one nightmare wilderness, and wreck of dead men's bones, this false modern world; and no rapt Ezekiel imaged to himself things sadder, more horrible and terrible, than the eyes of men, if they are awake, may now deliberately see."

And in these other words, what depth of truth is there not discernible! —

"Faith strengthens us, enlightens us, for all endeavors and endurances; with faith we can do all, and dare all, and life itself has a thousand times been joyfully given away. But the sum of man's misery is even this, that he feel himself crushed under the Juggernaut wheels, and know that Juggernaut is no divinity, but a dead mechanical idol."

And again, the angry voice breaks forth in sullen, almost despairing protest:—

"Not Godhead, but an iron, ignoble circle of necessity embraces all things; binds the youth of these times into a sluggish thrall, or else exasperates him into a rebel. Heroic action is paralyzed; for what worth now remains unquestionable with him? At the fervid period, when his whole nature cries aloud for action, there is nothing sacred under whose banner he can act; the course and kind and conditions of free action are all but indiscoverable. Doubt storms in on him through every avenue; inquiries of the deepest, painfullest sort must be engaged with; and the invincible energy of young years wastes itself in sceptical, suicidal cavillings, in passionate questionings of destiny, whence no answer will be returned."

The weakness, the shallowness, the misery, and selfishness which are the results of atheism and no-religion, are most clearly discerned and forcibly expressed by Carlyle. He sees that faith in something higher than himself is the one thing needful for man; that to live for vulgar objects and selfish ends is suicidal, is the denial and destruction of all that makes life worth having; and when men come with their schemes for making this earth a luxurious lubberland, where the brooks shall run wine, and the trees bend with ready-baked viands, and who bring their hand-lamp wherewith to dispel all darkness, he, without more ado, kicks his foot through it, and so leaves them and their paper contrivances. He has the gift of noble indignation. His very soul loathes all sham; he is the sworn enemy of cant, and holds sincerity to be the mother virtue. The sincere man is the divine man, the hero, the highest form which consciousness can assume. He comes to us at first hand, with tidings from the infinite unknown. The words he speaks are no other man's words; he comes from the inner fact of things, the heart of the world, the primal reality. That the hero have what men call faults is of small moment. We make too much of faults, says Carlyle. He is all fault who has no fault. Hence Mahomet, Luther, Cromwell, Rousseau, Burns, and Napoleon, are not simply men of genius and power, but they are messengers from heaven, true prophets, to be received and heard with all reverence and obedience; nay, to be worshipped in all sincerity. "And in this so despicable age of ours, — be the bounteous heavens ever thanked for it, — two heroes have nevertheless been found. Bonaparte walked through the war-convulsed world like an all-devouring earthquake, heaving, thundering, hurling kingdom over kingdom. Goethe was as the mild-shining, inaudible light, which, notwithstanding, can again make that chaos into a creation." And now the bounteous heavens have to this so despicable age vouchsafed a third hero, who is no other than Prince Bismarck; and, to crown the work of mercy, they have inspired Mr. Froude to reveal to his generation the heroic character and sublime worth of that much-abused and misunderstood demigod, Henry VIII. And so we have verified Carlyle's doctrine that the age of miracles is not past, but even now is.

Upon those who, in this modern world, are called religious, Carlyle pours, in boundless contempt, the full vials of his scorn and wrath. They are unveracities, chimeras, and semblances. Even the best of them keep trucking and trimming between worn-out symbols and hypocrisy. . . . "Birds of darkness are on the wing, spectres uproar, the dead walk, the living dream." The church-clothes, which once held and revealed to men's eyes the holy of holies, nothing else than the divine idea of the world, have now gone sorrowfully out at elbows. "Nay, far worse, many of them have become mere hollow shapes or masks, under which no living figure or spirit any longer dwells; but only spiders and unclean beetles, in horrid accumulation, drive their trade; and the mask still glares on you, with its glass eyes, in ghastly affectation of life." The religion of the Middle Ages is something quite different, nay, wholly opposite, a living and divine reality. "In those dark ages intellect could invent glass, which now she has enough ado to grind into spectacles. Intellect built not only churches, but a church, *the* church, based on this firm earth, yet reaching and leading up as high as heaven." This church was planted on the basis of fact, and built according to the laws of statics; and its heroes and prophets are troubled by no doubt, or any sort of doubt. Their "religion is not a diseased self-introspection, an agonizing inquiry; their duties are clear to them; the way of supreme good plain, indisputable, and they are travelling on it. Religion lies over *them* like an all-embracing heavenly canopy, like an atmosphere and life element, which is not spoken of, which, in all things, is presupposed without speech. Is not serene or complete religion the highest aspect of human nature, as serene cant or complete no-religion is the lowest and miserablest?"

"Our religion," he says, — speaking of what he calls "twelfth-century Catholicism," — "is not yet a horrible, restless doubt, still less a far horribler composed cant; but a great heaven-high unquestionability, encompassing, interpenetrating the whole of life."

In this old Church, planted on the basis of fact, built according to the laws of statics, heroes were not wanting. Here, for instance, is Abbot Samson: "The great antique heart, how like a child's in its simplicity, like a man's in its earnest solemnity and depth! Heaven lies over him wheresoever he goes or stands on the earth; making all the earth a mystic temple to him, the earth's business all a kind of worship. Heaven's splendor over his head, hell's darkness under his feet. It was not a dilettanteism this of Abbot Samson. It was a reality, and it is one. . . . This is Abbot Samson's Catholicism of the twelfth century. Alas! compared with any of the isms current in these poor days, what a thing!"

No one could have written a nobler history of Gregory VII. and his creative work than Carlyle; nor could he have found a grander hero; but his temper, like Milton's, led him rather to the great destroyers and mighty rebels, who walk through the convulsed world, upheaving, casting down, blowing to fragments men and their works.

In his doctrine of hero-worship there are doubtless elements of truth. The highest man is most like to God of anything that is visible in this earth. God himself has walked the earth clothed on with human nature, and of his divine gifts men are the ministers. The soul of man is more than any or all machinery. For man's sake was the Sabbath instituted, and for him all good and right institutions exist; not he for them. He is more than they. True religion must not only inspire reverence for man, but must produce heroic types of men, saints of God, who in strong and painful wrestlings with themselves and the spirits of darkness, struggle upwards to peace and light, leaving behind them a pathway, red with blood, but luminous; so that the multitudes who grope in the gloom of lower thoughts and loves, may not be left without some living testimony and effulgence of the higher world, for which all alike have been created. Even God's sacraments fall into disuse unless they are held in the hands of true, believing men. Reverence for those who are above us is not only a Christian virtue, but one which in this day has special need of being preached. And admiration, too, is wholesome and elevating. I admire the gift even where I condemn its use. The shallow spirit, which sees no greatness in man, and no great men, is irreligious. But Carlyle exaggerates the value and influence of hero-worship, and his ideal is not only false but immoral. "All religion," he says, "issues in due practical hero-worship. . . . Society is founded on hero-worship. . . . I seem to see in this indestructibility of hero-worship the everlasting adamant, lower than which the confused wreck of revolutionary things cannot fall." Of all this, what Carlyle would call attorney logic, and what here may fitly enough be called common sense, cannot approve. Nevertheless, even the logic-chopper must admit that it is fairly deducible from the premises. If man springs forth from the unconscious. as Carlyle holds, he can worship only himself; for the highest consciousness must necessarily think itself the absolute highest. In fact this whole system of hero-worship is but a development of Hegel's law of history, which is pantheistic. The ideal man, in this system, is in no true sense ideal. The sincere man is not the highest, best, wisest man; for fanaticism may be sincere as well as faith, and tyranny as well as justice. Moreover, sincerity, in Carlyle's thought, is synonymous with naturalness, and it may be urged with strong reason that goodness and virtue are not natural to man. Hence, Carlyle loses more and more all ground of difference between the *natural* and the *right;* his ideal grows less and less spiritual, until finally he fails to perceive any higher test of worth than sheer strength. Whatever can get upon its feet and stand there in spite of all enemies, is thereby self-consecrated, in his eyes, as a part of the eternal laws. The force which on its way to great achievements refuses to be controlled, the genius which acknowledges no law but itself, are not only wonderful but sacred and divine. Mahomet may be lustful, Cromwell cruel, Luther coarse and sensual, Burns a drunkard, Rousseau utterly abject; but to remark this is the most unmistakable proof that one is a blockhead. Let us bear in mind that Carlyle holds nature to be divine and all natural forces to be sacred, and we shall easily get at his point of view. These men are natural, and it is therefore simply absurd to suppose that they can be immoral. With what devout reverence and admiration does he not follow Mirabeau in his lust-defiled and madly reckless career? But the Count is natural, a swallower of formulas, a contemner of custom; and is not this divine, is it not the highest? Carlyle has some most eloquent passages on the quite infinite nature of duty, and Teufelsdröckh, even in the sorrowfulest wretchedness of unbelief, has still this light to convince him that the world is God's and not the devil's. But when we try to get at the exact import of duty, we cannot perceive that in his mind it means more than sincerity, naturalness. To this infinite nature of duty Mahomet, Cromwell, Mirabeau, and Frederick the Great were true; all men, in fact, it would seem, are true; for "man cannot but obey whatever he ought to obey."

In "Sartor Resartus" there is no more striking passage than the following: "There is in man a higher than love of happiness; he can do without happiness, and instead thereof find blessedness! . . . Love not pleasure, love God. This is the everlasting Yea, wherein all contradiction is solved; wherein whoso walks and works, it is well with him."

Love God, says Carlyle, but does he mean God? In the multitudinous writings which have poured from his pen since that precept was recorded, the command is not found, I think, a second time. Much and often has he spoken of the eternities, the immensities, the veracities, the silences, in whose presence we should stand in awe and wonder, with devout prostration of soul. Much and often too has he spoken of the unconscious, the unknown, the unnamable, the infinite nescience, the darkness, and mystery that shrouds man's whole life, lies everywhere, under his feet and among his hands. God's name, too, he has often since written; but a second time, as it is believed, he has not called upon men to love God. Whence this ominous silence? Love, in the human and only sense in which it has a meaning for us, is of persons and not of things. If God is the eternities, the immensities, the veracities, the unconscious, it would be most preposterous and absurd to ask us to love him. Wonder and prostration, self-annihilation, — all these, if you will, command, but not love, which cannot live except in the light of one who loves and knows. Do the eternities love me? Do the immensities know me? Does the unconscious care for me? I know the difficulties, I see the obscurities when we attempt to think of God as a person. The idea of God can be expressed in human language analogically only; yet is it undeniably and forever true that the highest being who knows and loves is the absolute highest. Eternities and immensities belong to Him, not He to them. Whatever allowance we may be disposed to make in consideration of the fact that Carlyle is a rhapsodist and a seer, it is impossible not to recognize that in his thinking God is not a person, and is not therefore the God whom

St. John declared to be Love. Carlyle has a disciple who is a most lucid and intelligible writer, whose thought is as transparent as the expression he gives it is precise; and he has translated his master's idea of God into the plainest and simplest language. "God," says Matthew Arnold, "is the eternal power, not ourselves, which makes for righteousness." ... "The stream of tendency by which all things fulfil the law of their being." And that this "eternal power," this "stream of tendency," is not a person who thinks and loves, he plainly tells us. The God of Christianity and of Judaism is, he says, only a magnified and non-natural man.

Here we have no mystic phrase, no uncertain light, no poetic symbolism; but the clear revelation of the eternities and the immensities. The word "God" is still employed because no other has such poetic and mysterious power over the human mind; and this is but an example of a general process in which the meaning of words is undergoing a complete transformation. Carlyle's God then does not love. He is "a force and thousandfold complexity of forces; a force which is not *we*. That is all, it is not we; it is altogether different from *us*. Force, force, everywhere force." Strength is the divine attribute; the strong are God's children; and to be weak is not only miserable, but immoral. This idea fills him with fierce thoughts and dark imaginings. The crashing of thrones, and the falling of altars, and the lurid light of burning cities, and the horrid din of murderous battle inspire him with wild delight. Force is building temples for its worship upon the wreck and ruin of all things. He loses, more and more, sympathy and tenderness, until he is wholly possessed by a sarcastic and gloomy indignation. The earth becomes a charnel-house, the dead uproar; the light of heaven dies out. They only are blessed who find rest in the bosom of the unconscious. The most fanatical hater of dogmas and creeds, he is become the most intolerant of thinkers. What he esteems a sham and chimera is so for the eternal laws. A symbol worn out for him is henceforth useless forever for all men. In such a temper contradictions must abound. He makes silence a god, and is himself a man of infinite words. The French Revolution fills him with a terrible glee, and yet he curses democracy. The end of life, he declares, with Goethe, to be action and not thought; and yet he keeps thinking and does not otherwise act. To reform a world, he well says, no wise man will undertake; and yet he chafes and is angry because the world has not been reformed by his preaching. If God is only the "stream of tendency," Renan is doubtless a true philosopher. "The thinker," he says, "believes that he has little right to direct the affairs of his planet; and, contented with the lot which has fallen to him, he accepts his impotence without regret. A spectator in the universe, he knows that the world belongs to him only as a subject of study; and though he were able to reform it, he would perhaps find it so curious as it is, that he would lack the courage to undertake the task."

Carlyle is not an original thinker. His theories are English interpretations of German thought; but interpretations which only a man of genius could have made. His influence and significance will be lightly estimated by those alone who have not understood him. His is the most important name in the English literature of this century, and the power which he has exercised upon the thought of England, and even of America, is vast and profound. In his earlier writings, in spite of the latent pantheism which has grown upon him with such fatal effect, he appealed to the higher and spiritual nature of man with an eloquence which reaches the inmost soul. He is a truer poet than Byron or Tennyson; a profounder thinker than Stuart Mill or Herbert Spencer; and a worthier historian than Macaulay or Froude. He has the most real and subtle humor; the pathos of a "divine despair;" infinite indignation; the holiest anger, and a seraph's loathing of mere matter; and by nature he is not without tenderness and the deepest sympathy.

His misfortune and defect is profound and radical scepticism concerning the highest truth. Greater and more awful than the eternities, the immensities, the unconscious, he can conceive of nothing. The many-colored picture of life is painted on a canvas of darkness, and in the background there hovers a region of doubt which thought cannot possibly transform into certainty. He fails to perceive that what forces us to recognize a reality beneath appearances, proclaims also the presence of mind in the laws and harmonies of nature. The fearful and infinite force overwhelms him, and the supreme and central power of love and wisdom is not felt. Hence we find him still, as his disciple has sung of himself —

>"Wandering between two worlds, one dead,
> The other powerless to be born."

After all that can be said, has been said, in praise of Force, this still remains to be said, that it cannot be loved. And yet except in trustful love man finds no peace and no blessedness.

"Unhappy men," said St. Teresa, "who do not love!"

## CHAPTER VI.

### CULTURE AND RELIGION.

*The aids to noble life lie all within.*—MATTHEW ARNOLD.

THE simple and comprehensive idea of education includes within itself almost everything. It is as many-sided as human nature, and its limits are as wide as the capacities of the soul, which in its hopes, desires, and aspirations is infinite. All things have an educational value, and that man is educable is the great and guiding fact in history. Forms of government, laws, social customs, literature, industrial arts, climate, and soil not only educate, but are esteemed according to the kind of education which they give. Whatever tends to make one more than he is or to hinder him from being less than he is, is a part of education. The various races of men are doubtless unlike in their natural endowments, but they differ far more widely by reason of the dissimilar educational influences which have acted upon them.

It may be affirmed with truth that our good qualities are acquired.

We are taught to be modest, truthful, brave, gentle, humane, as we are taught to speak a language. Excellence is thus a triumph over nature, and virtue is the result of victories over instinctive passion. The tendency so common in our day to exalt instinct, almost to consecrate it, springs from an optimistic theory which is utterly at variance with the facts. The wise man does not follow nature but subdues it into conformity with reason; though to do this he must, of course, work in accordance with the laws of nature. The first and deepest element in the life of the individual as of the race is religious faith, which consequently is the chief and highest instrument of education. Religion is man's supreme effort to rise above nature and above his natural self. It gives him a definite aim and an absolute ideal. "Be ye perfect," it says, "as your Heavenly Father is perfect." It constitutes him a dweller in a world where mere utility has no place. It gives him high thoughts of himself, and thereby exalts his aims and heightens his standards of conduct. It makes him feel that to be true, to be good, to be beautiful, is most desirable, even though no practical gain or use should thence follow. It turns his thoughts to spiritual worth and diminishes his estimate of what is accidental and phenomenal. It addresses itself to the soul, and seeks to give it that pre-eminence which is the condition of all progress; for, "by the soul only shall the nations be great and free." It proclaims the paramount worth of right conduct, which alone brings a man at peace with himself, and thus makes possible the harmonious development of his being. Little cause for wonder is there that everywhere in all time priests should be the first teachers of the race; that poetry, and music, and painting, and sculpture, and architecture should first become possible when the creative voice of faith in the unseen commands them to exist. But upon this it is not my purpose now to dwell, and I merely intimate that true religion, as it appeals to all man's highest faculties with supreme power, must necessarily promote true culture. The direct aim of religion, however, is not to produce culture, nor is it the immediate aim of culture to produce religion; and it may, therefore, happen that they come in conflict. I take the matter seriously, and have not the faintest desire to join in the easy sneer with which this word *culture* is often received. That in the mouths of the frivolous and the vulgar it should be no better than cant, is only what may happen to any word which such persons take up, and it were wiser to reflect that the ideal of culture has exercised an irresistible fascination over many of the most finely endowed minds that have ever lived.

The word itself may not indeed be the best; but it seems to serve the purpose better than any other which we who speak English possess. They who propose culture to us as something desirable, would have us aim at a full and harmonious development of our nature, greater freedom from narrowness and prejudice, more disinterested and expansive sympathies, flexibility and openness of mind, courtesy and gentleness, and whatever else goes to form the idea of a liberal education. And if we ask them what end we may expect to gain by following this advice, we betray our inability to appreciate their words. Culture is an end in itself, and brings its own reward. It is good to have a trained and flexible mind, wide and refined sympathies. Just as those who are truly religious do not value their faith for any worldly advantage which it may give them, so the disciples of culture cannot consider the pursuit of excellence as a means of success. To aim at such a result would be to deny the virtue of culture. They are little concerned with the usefulness of knowledge. The knowledge is more than its use, and they choose rather to be intelligent than to be rich or powerful or in office.

To urge the pursuit of learning with a view to money-making is apostasy from light, is desertion to the enemies of the soul. This opinion, it is needless to say, is in open conflict with our American notions of education. Utility is our guiding principle in this matter, and to say of any kind of knowledge that it is not useful is to condemn it. The best defence which we can set up in behalf of religion itself is to prove that it promotes the general welfare; that it is useful, not that it is true. Hardly any man with us is able to rise above this spirit, which controls not only our elementary, but equally our higher education. We universally regard knowledge as a means to worldly success. A certain mental training we hold to be essential, and those who go beyond this study with a view to entering some one of the professions. But to study for even a learned profession is not the way to get a liberal education; for this highest culture comes when the mind is disciplined for its own sake, and not with the view to narrow and fit it to any trade or business. Hence, it not unfrequently happens that successful professional men are almost wholly lacking in general intelligence, mental flexibility, and wide sympathies. And this is even used as an argument against culture.

That we take a utilitarian view of education

is neither accidental nor unintentional. It is the view which our history suggests and seems to justify, and it is the one which we as a people have deliberately chosen to adopt. And in the estimation of a very great many persons the result is satisfactory. The aim is not exalted, and it has been attained with remarkable rapidity and ease. Hence we are self-complacent and inclined to boastfulness. We point with pride to our vast population, to the boundless extent of territory which we have subdued and forced to yield up its wealth, to the roads and cities which we have built, to the schools which are within the reach of all and are the same for all, to the industrial and commercial enterprise which enables us to compete successfully in the markets of the world with the oldest and richest nations, to the inventive genius which leads in the application of mechanical contrivances to the production of personal and social comfort, and, to crown our happiness, we are the freest of all peoples. That we are faultless no one pretends to claim; but our achievements are so real and valuable, that we should not be slow to believe that the methods which have enabled us to accomplish so much will give us also the power to overcome the dangers which may threaten our peace and progress. Our aims are mechanical, and in congratulating ourselves upon the success with which we attain them we lose sight of the fact that these aims ought not to be pursued as ends in themselves. Freedom and wealth, like railroads and telegraphs, are means and not ends. Their value is not in themselves, but in what is made possible through them; and it is the office of culture to force people to recognize this. The cultivated mind is smitten with the love of an internal and spiritual beauty, and holds machinery cheap. It is bent upon seeing things as they are; it looks through marble walls and gaudy liveries and the smoke of factories, and will not be content until it discovers what beauty and truth, if any, are hidden under these shows. It is wholly free from the superstition of wealth and success. If the rich man is ignorant, coarse, and narrow, he is a beggar in the eyes of culture. Fond parents in this land find great comfort in the thought that their boy may one day be President of the United States; but if the President is a sot or a boor, culture will ignore him though he should hold office for life.

We cannot laugh at culture to any good purpose, for it has the spiritual mind which judges all things. To the opinions of the vulgar it gives no heed, and they who have insight are reverent, seeing that it is good. It can be indifferent even to fame. Here again we may remark that its unworldly temper and spiritual standard of perfection bring it into friendly relation with religion. Culture is concerned with the formation of the mind and the character, and values all things with reference to this end. It does not despise temporal and mechanical benefits, but seeks to turn them to the account of the soul. The man is more than his money, or his office, or his trade. Wealth is good in that it gives freedom and independence, the opportunity for self-improvement. The worth of all this money-getting industrialism which absorbs our life is in the preparation which it makes for culture. The test of civilization is the degree of human perfection which it produces. To dwell with complacency upon the thought of our cities, railroads, and wealth, is to be narrow and vulgar. We are not concerned with wood, and stone, and iron, but with man. What kind of man will this social mechanism shape? This is what we are interested to know, and this is what culture would have us keep in view. There are many intelligent, and otherwise not unfriendly persons, who placing themselves at this standpoint, find it impossible to look with enthusiasm or even complacency upon our American life. Renan, for instance, with whom the idea of culture is supreme, takes no pains to conceal his opinion of us. "The countries," he says, "which, like the United States, have created a considerable popular instruction, without any serious higher education, will long have to expiate this fault by their intellectual mediocrity, their vulgarity of manners, their superficial spirit, their lack of general intelligence."

Again: "The ideal of American society is further removed than that of any other from the ideal of a society governed by science. The principle that society exists only for the welfare and freedom of the individuals of which it is composed, would seem to be contrary to the plans of nature, which takes care of the species, but sacrifices the individual. It is greatly to be feared lest the final outcome of this kind of democracy be a social state in which the degenerate masses will have no other desire than to indulge in the ignoble pleasures of the lower and vulgar man." And Renan thinks it probable that the senseless vanity of a population which has received elementary instruction, will make it unwilling to contribute to the maintenance of an education superior to its own; and he, therefore, has little hope that democracy will prove favorable to culture and the production of great men, which, in his opinion, is the end for which the human race exists. With this view of American life Matthew Arnold coincides. The circumstances of the case force him to think that America, the chosen home of newspapers and politics, is without general intelligence; "and that in the things of the mind, and in culture and totality, America, instead of surpassing us all, falls short." The cause of this he finds not so much in our democratic form of government as in the inherited tendencies of the people of the United States, which issues from the English Puritan middle class and reproduces its narrow conception of man's spiritual range.

Let us receive with equanimity and good-nature the criticism which finds us so greatly deficient in knowledge and refinement. Our ability to do this is of itself encouraging. The era in which it was possible to think that whatever is American is excellent has fortunately passed, and a greater familiarity with the history, the literature, and the manners of other nations has taken the freshness from our self-conceit. The sweet uses of adversity too have taught us most admirable lessons. Every man may have a vote, and every child may go to school, and the time may still be out of joint; the increase of national wealth need not protect the multitude from poverty and suffering, and the growth of intelligence may coexist with the decay of morals and the loss of faith.

"It is not fatal to Americans," says Arnold, "to have no religious establishments, and no effective centres of high culture; but it is fatal to them to be told by their flatterers, and to believe, that they are the most intelligent people in the world, when of intelligence in the true and fruitful sense of the word, they even singularly, as we have seen, come short."

Admitting all, even the worst that can be said of us on this point, our very enemies must nevertheless concede that the preparations for a higher culture have been made by us and exist under altogether favorable conditions. Great fault may be justly found with our whole educational mechanism. The colleges and universities are doubtless imperfect enough and often obstacles to the development of intelligence. But the remedy is in our hands.

Our wealth and industrialism place within easy reach whatever can be accomplished by money, and there are no difficulties which may not be overcome by earnest faith in the ideal which culture presents. The important question for us is whether this ideal ought to excite our admiration and love. A very great number of sincere and enlightened men, representing conflicting tendencies and opposite schools of thought, look upon the ideal of culture as false and hurtful to the best interests of man; and the objections which they urge are numerous and weighty. The masses of mankind, they say, have neither the opportunity nor the desire for culture; and this is fortunate, for devotion to this ideal has an unmistakable tendency to diminish zeal for the general welfare. The men of culture hold themselves aloof from the crowd and take no interest in the practical questions of the day. They live in a dreamland of poesy, and in the consciousness of their inability to help forward any good cause content themselves with criticism, which unsettles convictions and weakens the zest for action. They preach loud enough that the end of life is an act and not a thought, and yet both their example and their teaching tend to obscure all the ways of life in which men are accustomed to labor. Goethe writes poetry and preserves his philosophic serenity in the midst of the appalling calamities of his country, of which he seems to be altogether oblivious. Carlyle, through half a century, chides his fellow-men, accepts neither faith nor science, neither acts himself nor points out to others how they may labor to good purpose. Arnold frankly admits that he has no desire to see men of culture intrusted with power, and were he consulted by his countrymen on questions of actual moment he could only repeat the precept of Socrates, "Know thyself." When France lay crushed and bleeding at the feet of Germany, Renan withdrew to a quiet retreat to compose Platonic dialogues, in which he gives expression to his contempt for the crowd and his distrust of all the popular movements of the age. Culture thus seems to produce a sceptical and effeminate habit of mind which is incompatible with strong and abiding convictions, and consequently destructive of resolution and enthusiasm, without which man cannot accomplish any great purpose in life; and Mr. Frederic Harrison may not be wholly mistaken in thinking that the men of culture are the only class of responsible beings in the community who cannot with safety be intrusted with power. This he says of England, and without reference to America, where this class can hardly be said to exist at all; and the apprehension of their getting into power need not, therefore, be a cause of anxiety to our statesmen, whose mental resources, even as things are, seem to be not more than sufficient to meet the demands which are made upon them. The believers in culture, it is further urged, are propagandists of a cosmopolitan and non-national spirit, which undermines patriotism, directs attention to an impossible ideal, and disenchants men of their inherited character, which, whatever may be its faults, is the essential basis of virtue and excellence. The education derived from the national genius, like that of the family, cannot be supplied by any other agency, and the cosmopolitanism which ignores this must necessarily tend to create a temper like that of the ideal Epicurean, who is described as indifferent to public affairs and the fate of empires, and not subject to any such weakness as pity for the poor or jealousy of the rich. In this view, then, culture is destructive of patriotism.

Other objections are urged against its ethical character. Culture, it is said, is only a refined epicureanism. Its aim is to educate man so as to fit him for the enjoyment of the greatest possible pleasure. It shrinks from vice, not because it is evil, but because it is gross and disgusting. The men of culture, like the ancient Greeks, are without the sense of sin, and consequently at best have but a conventional morality.

Aristophanes was not more pagan than Goethe, who is the typical representative of the new religion. He it is who taught that to be beautiful is higher than to be good; and his denial of sin is implied in the doctrine that repentance is wrong. He assumes that there is no objective standard of right and wrong. Man is a law unto himself, and the pursuit of perfection is the effort to bring all his faculties into free and unhindered play. That which I feel to be true is true for me; that which I feel to be good is good for me; and therefore creeds and dogmas, whether religious or philosophic, cease to have either life or meaning as soon as the time-spirit has flown from them. The web of life is woven of necessity and chance; we must yield to destiny, and seek to make the most of chance. Happiness is to be sought, not in the fulfilment of duty, but in the sweetness and light which are the results of the complete and harmonious development of our nature. "Woe be to every kind of education," says Goethe, "which destroys the means of obtaining true culture, and points our attention to the end instead of securing our happiness on the way." The philosophy of culture is, then, it would appear, only another form of utilitarianism, and tacitly assumes that greatest-happiness principle against which it so loudly protests.

It, in fact, looks upon this life as alone real and enjoyable, and considers him a madman who troubles himself here in the hope of obtaining blessedness hereafter. Morality, consequently, is nothing absolute, and whatever secures our "happiness on the way" is good. The point sought to be made is this: that, as culture results intellectually in universal criticism and doubt, so it morally ends in unlimited indulgence. The vulgar herd, finding no delight in the refined and studied pleasures of the cultivated, will have no other way of showing its appreciation of their theories than by wallowing in Epicurus's sty. And this, indeed, is the history of culture amongst all peoples. We know from Aristophanes what was the moral condition of the age of Pericles; and he ascribes the frightful degeneracy from the standard of conduct which made the men who fought and won at Marathon to what he most aptly calls the " new education," or in the language of our time, modern culture. The same story is repeated in Rome. Virtue and public spirit flourished in the midst of poverty and rustic manners; but when conquered Greece with the silken cords of culture led her captors captive, together with letters and refinement every kind of corruption was introduced into the State; and the Latin classics almost universally attribute the ruin of their country to this cause. Sallust considers a taste for painting as a vice no less than drunkenness; and Horace abounds in praise of the rigid virtue and simple ways of the fathers. And in modern times the age of Leo X. was an era of moral degeneracy, and that of Louis XIV. was immediately followed by the most humiliating and disgraceful epoch in French history; while in England, culture, as represented by the court of Charles II., fostered the most loathsome and hideous sensuality. Germany's culture period, too, is one of moral paralysis, and it is not surprising that it should have created the philosophy of hate and despair as taught by Schopenhauer and Von Hartmann. Goethe himself may inspire admiration and enthusiasm, but not perfect respect.

It is further urged that this historical relationship between culture and licentiousness is founded in the nature of things; that polite literature and the elegant arts necessarily tend to create frivolous and effeminate habits of thought and feeling, because they separate the sentiment from the deed, whereas the end of feeling is to impel us to act. To luxuriate therefore in fine sentiments, noble thoughts, and the elegancies of style, and to rest in this indulgence is of itself immoral. The springs of action are thereby perverted from their proper use, and a character is developed like that of novel-readers who weep over the misfortunes of imaginary heroes, and spurn the wretched from their door. The lovers of culture themselves recognize the evil and the danger, and hence they vociferously preach the necessity of action; but in vain, as their own example shows. They give us fine theories, but have no hope of realizing them; which is not surprising, for the habit of considering things from every point of view, and of weighing all that can be said for and against every opinion, begets a sophistical and hesitating disposition, which as a matter of course renders action distasteful, and moreover warps the practical judgment and unfits it for deciding upon any right course of conduct. A dreamer is not a man of action, and the work of the world is not done by critics.

St. Paul's examples of men who wrought great things by faith may be generalized and applied universally. All heroic conduct springs from the confidence which comes of faith. Knowledge does not suffice; for what will be the outcome of a given series of human acts cannot be known, and must therefore be taken on trust. Men who perform grandly see what ought to be done and move forward; that is, they trust their intuitions, and not the analysis of a critical survey of the situation. At the battle of Lodi, Napoleon said the bridge must be taken; his officers declared it impregnable; he unsheathed his sword and passed over it behind the fleeing enemy. Culture is dilettanteism. It may fill up an idle hour, but is as impotent to lead the world as millinery. In fact, Arnold himself seems to perceive that it is just here that the special weakness of the new philosophy is revealed. The men of culture have failed conspicuously in conduct. They are unable even to subdue "the great faults of our animality." "They have failed in morality, and morality is indispensable." He insists again and again upon the paramount importance of conduct, and for the development of this ethical character he trusts to religion and not to culture. Hence though for him God is only "the stream of tendency," he will not give up the Bible. He throws aside indeed the whole dogmatic basis upon which the Bible rests, and yet would still seem to think that it is possible to preserve its moral teaching; and this leads us to another objection which is urged by the opponents of culture, namely, that it is irreligious. That this objection is not unfounded appears plainly to follow from what has already been said; for if culture fatally ends in universal criticism and immorality it is obviously in open conflict with religion. There is, it is true, an apparent similarity in their aims and ideals. Both propose perfection as the end to be sought for, and both place this perfection in an inward spiritual state, and not in any outward condition; and neither therefore looks upon material progress with the complacency which is so natural to the mere worldling. A deeper view, however, will discover the latent antagonism. The perfection at which culture aims is purely natural and has reference to this life alone. It loves excellence rather than virtue, and is enamoured of beauty rather than of goodness. Religion emphasizes the evil of sin; culture its grossness. The thoughts of the religious are with God, while the lovers of culture are occupied with themselves; and hence humility is the attitude of the one, and pride of the other. Self-denial is accepted by culture only as a means to higher and purer pleasure; by religion it is inculcated as the proof of love. Culture believes in this life only; religion in the life to come. And finally, culture looks upon itself as an end; but in the eyes of religion it can be at best merely a means.

As it is not my purpose to enter a plea on behalf of culture, I shall be at no pains to attempt an answer in detail to all these objections. That many of them at least are not captious, but are based upon real views of the subject, I am ready to admit; and nevertheless the case of those who dispute the validity of the inference which is drawn is, as I take it, not desperate. To those who urge that culture is cosmopolitan and weakens the spirit of patriotism, the reply may be made that an exaggerated nationalism has been the cause of numberless woes to the human race. This is the stronghold of war and of all the train of evils which follow in its wake; this is the source of that restrictive legislation which has interfered with free trade and built barriers in the way of progress; this is the foment of that fatal prejudice which has nurtured a narrow conceit, that shuts the national mind of each country against the world's experience.

The Christian doctrine of the brotherhood of all men, and of one world-wide spiritual kingdom in which all may receive the rights of citizenship, would seem to point toward a social state in which differences of race and country, if not obliterated, will at least remain comparatively inoperative. That the men of culture would make but sorry statesmen or leaders of party we may grant. But a poet is not found fault with because he is not a metaphysician, nor is a general criticised for lack of taste in the fine arts. It is quite as important surely that there should be calm and enlightened thinkers as that there should be sturdy and indefatigable workers; and precisely where men are busiest with their temporal projects and mechanical contrivances, it is well that there should be found those who assume a loftier tone and point to higher aims. Every supreme mind, like the loftiest mountain peaks, rises into a region where it dwells, far above the storm-cloud, in serene solitude; and, therefore, is it said that genius is melancholy. The most perfect culture also partakes of this loneliness, and is ill at ease in the crowd; but this only serves to enhance the value of the criticism which it pronounces upon the common ways and aims of men. He who, free from the passion and blinding dust of the conflict, surveys the field from an eminence, sees many things which are hidden from the eyes of the combatants. It is the fault of the eager rivalry of busy life that it leaves no time for calm reflection, and hence active workers grow narrow, and would bend the universe to their little schemes. The salvation of society is made to depend upon the crotchet of a politician or upon the opening up of a new market for some article of commerce, or it is held to be within the competency of a school system to bring on the millennium. It is certainly of the first importance that men be fed, and clothed, and governed; but, as Goethe says, "the useful encourages itself, for the crowd produce it and none can dispense with it; the beautiful needs encouragement, for few can create it, and it is required by many." If the men of culture do not act, they at least furnish the means of activity to others. The old alchemists were no better than dreamers and idlers, but to them we are indebted for our physical science. It is easier to act than to think; and hence the world abounds in busy men, whereas a real thinker is hardly to be met with. Should we then employ all our efforts to stimulate an activity which is already feverish, and do nothing to encourage wider and profounder habits of thought? To take the lowest view, it will hardly be denied that the power to think correctly is useful. Idealists are often laughed at in their own day; but the dreams of the present not unfrequently become the recognized principles of action of the future. The common man, of course, living in the present, is impatient to see his labors bear immediate fruit; and a vulgar generation attaches little value to the good which can be enjoyed only by those who come after it; but without self-denial neither wisdom nor virtue can exist, and to aim at the reward which comes of right conduct is the certain way to disappointment.

The charge that culture has an immoral tendency is more serious, and possibly not so easily set aside, for history seems to bear out the assertion that ages of luxury and refinement have been invariably remarkable for licentiousness of manners. It is plain, however, that the vices as well as the virtues of a civilized people differ from those of barbarians. The highway robber is generally no sybarite. Civilization brings large bodies of men together in cities, encourages industry, protects wealth, creates classes that abound in opulence and leisure, and it consequently offers opportunities for the indulgence of effeminate and luxurious habits. The spirit of an age of refinement is humane and merciful. Its tastes are nice and its pleasures attractive. The tempers of men are softened, and war itself smooths its rugged front, and is waged without vindictive cruelty. The weak are protected, the orphan is cared for, and the poor find sympathy. The man of culture sins by over-refinement, the vulgar man by excess in indulgence. Savages and barbarians are not epicures, but they are the slaves of gluttony and drunkenness to a greater extent than the civilized races. Again, venality and bribery will not be common in an age in which the ambitious and covetous find it easier to attain their ends by violence. It must be borne in mind too that the literature of an age of culture generally becomes classic, and hence the vices of those ages are made immortal, while the memory of the crimes of barbarians perishes. And there is ever a spirit of restlessness and discontent in an epoch of refinement, which causes men to yield more readily to the natural propensity to depreciate the present and unduly exalt the past; and it so happens that its vices are precisely those which lend themselves most effectively to the purpose of the satirist. A few examples of cruelty and licentiousness are fastened upon, and are so perverted as to be made to appear to be the rule to which they are only exceptions.

To consider the subject, then, apart from the question as to the relation which exists between religious faith and morality, and this is the view we now take of it, it does not appear that a state of culture is more favorable to vice than barbarism. It would seem on the contrary that knowledge, refinement, and industry tend to make men virtuous. If we hear less of the crimes of savage and barbarous peoples it is not because they do not abound, but because they are not recorded, or when recorded repel us, since a cultivated mind can find no pleasure in reading of rapine, and murder, and brutish orgies; whereas, unfortunately, such is the weakness of man, when sin loses its grossness it seems even to those who are not depraved to lose something of its evil.

But after all has been said it must be confessed that the history of culture does not justify us in thinking that it is able to create a pure and genuine morality. At best it but throws the cloak of decency over the ulcer which it is powerless to heal. Ascetic writers tell us that in order to combat sin successfully we must have a real abhorrence of it, and this culture lacks. With it virtue is a point of good taste, and vice want of breeding; and it does not hate the evil, but fears the shame and confusion of detection. This, I say, is the ethical character of historical culture, and I now proceed to examine whether it is a defect inherent in the nature of culture, or an accident attributable to the conditions under which it has been developed.

Culture, in the modern sense of the word, and considered apart from the influence of Christianity, is derived from Athens, the city of mind and the world's first university. No people has ever equalled the Athenian in mental versatility, grace, penetration, and originality. The proverb "To think is difficult; to act, easy" seems to be untrue in their case. Thought was as natural and as easy to them as to breathe, and there is hardly an intellectual or poetical conception in modern literature which may not be found, in germ at least, even in the comparatively small portion of their writings that has come down to us; and their language is still the most perfect instrument of thought known to men. They were, and to a great extent still are, the teachers of the civilized world in philosophy, eloquence, poetry, and art; and they have, therefore, necessarily exerted, whether for good or evil, a vast ethical influence. Now to the Greek, virtue and beauty are identical. His religion is the worship of the beautiful; and the good is the fair, the harmonious, the musical. The very name which he gave to the universe indicated that it revealed itself to his mind primarily under the aspect of harmony and proportion; and hence for conscience he substituted taste, a kind of exquisite sense of the graceful and the decorous, and his religion embodied itself in art. His sacred books were poems, his temples, which were models of grace and symmetry, were open to the heavens and bathed in the cheerful light of day, and when he offered sacrifice and prayer he was crowned with flowers and quaffed the golden wine with song and dance. In his maturity he is only a handsome youth in whose veins the current of life is full and strong. He walks in a perennial spring, and the flowers bloom wherever he goes, and the air trills with the matin songs of birds. He lives in a world of delights and dreads nothing but death. He has no thought of sin, the very gods love what he loves and think no wrong. And when he praises virtue it is because it is noble, and beautiful, and full of pleasant sweetness. It is a fine figure, graceful and fair as a statue of Pentelic marble chiselled by the hand of Phidias. Unfortunately, a theory based upon the assumption that to do right is to do only what is pleasant will not fit into a world which has been wrenched from its original harmony. The sense of the beautiful was soon sunk in sensuous voluptuousness, and Athens has left us nothing to admire except her genius. And yet the ideal of life which her great minds have traced out for us is so noble, so generous, that we are hardly surprised that its winning grace and brightness should create a kind of worship in the sensitive souls of poets and artists, and thus impress ineffaceably its own fair features upon the culture of all succeeding ages. But as this ideal is without moral force and the seriousness of character which is thence derived, it is, like many fairest things, frail and unsuited to the stern work of a world where self-conquest is the price of victory. There is want of correspondence between the inward strength and the outward form, and in thinking of this noble dream of genius we can but repeat the poet's lament for Italy: —

"Italia! oh, Italia, thou who hast
 The fatal gift of beauty, which became
A funeral dower of present woes and past,
 On thy sweet brow is sorrow ploughed by shame."

Culture is akin to poetry, but life is mostly prose and must rest upon a more substantial basis. Is it not possible, then, we ask, to bring to the help of this fine and artistic ideal of human perfection some force, not its own, from which it may derive the strength not to yield to the fatality of its natural bent? In other words,— can religion, whose dominant idea is morality, be brought into friendly relationship with culture, the ruling thought of which is beauty, or to use the accepted phrase, sweetness and light? In introducing the present examination I stated that there need be no antagonism between true religion and true culture, and I now find that I am called upon to defend or else to withdraw this affirmation. "Deny thyself" is the word of Christ; "Think of living" is the precept of culture; and certainly the self-indulgent and pleasure-seeking life of the Greek is the very opposite of the ideal which is presented to the Christian. The one looks upon this earth as a garden of delight; the other has no abiding city here, but passes as a pilgrim, who in the midst of gay scenes is restless, for his thoughts are with those he loves in the far-off home. The Greek rests in nature and worships it; the Christian looks through nature to God, and places it beneath his feet. To the one the cross is foolishness; to the other it is the power and wisdom of God. That culture is not Christianity, needs no proof. Its whole history is characterized by the absence of that moral earnestness which is the very soul of religious faith, and it therefore lacks an element which is the chief constituent of human perfection. If culture is not Christianity, is Christianity culture; or is it also partial and without the power to create a fully-developed humanity? This is the charge that Arnold, while frankly confessing the shortcomings of culture, brings against religion, which, he thinks, takes a narrow view of man, and is destined finally to be transformed and governed by the Hellenic idea of beauty and of a human nature perfect on all its sides. His criticisms on this subject, which are aimed chiefly at the Protestant theory of Christianity, are sprightly and entertaining. The Pilgrim Fathers, he says, and their standard of perfection are rightly judged "when we figure to ourselves Shakespeare or Virgil — *souls* in whom sweetness and light and all that in human nature is most humane were eminent — accompanying them on their voyage, and think what intolerable company Shakespeare and Virgil would have found them."

"And the work," he says, "which we collective children of God do, our grand centre of life, our *city* which we have builded for us to dwell in, is London! London, with its unutterable external hideousness, and with its internal

canker of *publice egestas, privatim opulentia,*—
to use the words which Sallust puts into Cato's
mouth about Rome,— unequalled in the world!
The word, again, which we children of God
speak, the voice which most hits our collective
thought, the newspaper with the largest circulation in England, nay, with the largest circulation
in the whole world, is the *Daily Telegraph!*"
Real Protestantism, Arnold thinks, is not merely
lacking in sweetness and light, but is positively
hideous and grotesque; and he remarks that
there are things in which defect of beauty is
defect of truth. "Behavior," he says, "is not
intelligible, does not account for itself to the
mind and show the reason for its existing, unless
it is beautiful. The same with discourse, the
same with song, the same with worship,— all of
them modes in which man proves his activity
and expresses himself. To think that when one
produces in these what is mean or vulgar or
hideous, one can be permitted to plead that one
has that within which passes show, it is abhor-
rent to the nature of Hellenism to concede."
Again: "Instead of our 'one thing needful'
justifying in us vulgarity, hideousness, ignorance, violence,— our vulgarity, hideousness,
ignorance violence, are really so many touch-
stones which try our one thing needful, and
which prove that, in the state at any rate in

which we ourselves have it, it is not all we want."

Arnold's culturism is not original, any more than Carlyle's mysticism. The one and the other are only English interpretations of German and French thought, and Arnold himself would be the first to acknowledge this; nay, he has confessed as much in the following words: "Now, as far as real thought is concerned, thought which affects the best reason and spirit of man, the scientific or the imaginative thought of the world, the only thought which deserves speaking of in this solemn way, America has up to the present time been hardly more than a province of England, and even now would not herself claim to be more than abreast of England; and of this only real human thought, English thought itself is not just now, as we must all admit, the most significant factor." To get a satisfactory view of his position we must, therefore, pass over to the continent of Europe, with the understanding, however, that no attempt be made to reduce his views to a system. Lacordaire declared that, by the grace of God, he abhorred the commonplace; and Arnold, with or without such grace, abhors all systems, whether mechanical, political, metaphysical, or theological. His chapters on "The God of Metaphysics," in which by a few simple etymologies and with perfect *gaîté de cœur* he dissipates into thin air the profoundest thought of the greatest minds who have ever lived, will doubtless be immortal as a curiosity of literature. He has no system, but he has a method, which is that of the modern critical school, which assumes as fundamental the celebrated maxim of Protagoras, that "man is the measure of all things." The eternal, the all-perfect does not exist except as a mode of thought, which is simply the effort of the thinker to posit himself as an absolute principle and to refer all things to himself. True and fruitful thought consequently is not that which is in accord with any definite and fixed object, but that which moves in harmony with the stream of tendency and is carried upon the out-spread wings of the time-spirit. There is, in fact, no truth, but only opinions; no color, but only shades, and we must, therefore, abandon as utterly hopeless the effort to know things in themselves, and content ourselves with studying their evolutions; throw aside metaphysics and psychology as the childish toys of an infantine race, and take up in their stead history and criticism. The characteristic mark of the true critic is a disinterested curiosity, and that this word has in English only a bad and feminine sense, Arnold thinks a grievance. The critic does not search for the truth which does not exist, but he seeks to supple his mind so that he may be able to see things on all sides, and remain an enlightened and impartial spectator of the dissolving views of a world which is only an eternal flux; and that his appreciation may be the keener, he becomes a part of all that he beholds. He is a citizen of the universe, and moves in calm indifference in all times and places, amongst all religions and philosophies. He, however, has an unmistakable penchant for religious discussions, as though after having denied the reality of God and the soul he were still haunted by their phantoms. He is capable, even as Renan, Ewald, and Arnold have shown, of a sort of poetical and sad devoutness, which, if it were not ridiculous, would be pathetic. He has no toleration for the unintelligent and vulgar rage against religion which is manifested by popular liberalism and atheism. When Clifford breaks out into violent invectives and calls Christianity an awful plague, Arnold in a sweet and winning tone gives him a gentle rebuke, though his anger is not aroused in this instance as it was by Bishop Wilberforce when he spoke of laboring for the honor and glory of God. "One reads it all," he says, "half sighing, half smiling, as the declamation of a clever and confident youth, with the hopeless inexperience, irredeemable by any cleverness of his age. Only when one is young and headstrong can one thus prefer bravado to experience, can one stand by the Sea of Time, and instead of listening to the solemn and rhythmical beat of its waves, choose to fill the air with one's own whoopings to start the echo." His writings, in fact, he takes the trouble to inform us, have no other object than to save the Christian religion from its friends, who by teaching that it is inseparable from specific dogmas are placing it and themselves in fatal antagonism to the time-spirit and the critic, who is its prophet. In reality the essential thought of culturism, as conceived by the school from which Arnold has drawn his opinions, does not differ from that of mysticism or any of the other forms of modern pantheism. Its distinguishing characteristic is found not in its idea but in its temper. As an intellectual theory it is purely pantheistic. It regards the universe as its own final and efficient cause, and maintains that it is absurd to affirm the existence of any being distinct from the cosmos; and hence it teaches that God is not a person who knows and loves, but a "stream of tendency," a law, a modality; or, to take Renan's definition, the form under which we conceive the ideal, as space and time are the forms under which matter is made intelligible to us. God is only the category of the ideal, and when the German pantheists declare that man makes God, that man creates God in thinking Him, they do not mean to blaspheme or to be smart, but merely pronounce a logical conclusion from their own theories. But when men who make God a modality, a form of thought, talk about saving the Bible and Christianity, we have a perfect right to turn away from them as solemn triflers in a matter which, least of all, admits of such proceeding. The idea then of culturism is pantheistic, which is the equivalent of atheistic; and as atheism is the negation of religion, any attempt to bring about an alliance between religion and culture, upon the intellectual basis offered by the critical school, is preposterous, for the simple reason that the hypothesis which this school accepts as true makes religion impossible. When Renan and Arnold assure us that they do not seek to weaken the religious sentiment but to purify it, we can but liken them to a physician who in order to purge out the humors of the blood should think it necessary first to destroy life.

A religion of sweetness and light in a Godless world, which crushes beneath the iron wheel of fate the weak and the helpless, and has no favors except for the strong, is a piece of Mephistophelean irony, compared with which the pessimism of Schopenhauer is as soothing as the quiet landscape to one who flies from the feverish life of the noisy crowd. Is it not enough that these men are persuaded that there is no God and no soul? Why should they come to us proclaiming that the earth is only a charnel-house, and in the same breath grow eloquent over the refreshing and refining influence which this discovery of theirs must have upon those who are able to appreciate its importance? To be just, however, I must leave Arnold to bear alone the burden of this officious piety. One must be an Englishman to be able to deny God and still continue to preach with all the unction of a Methodist exhorter. Renan is consistent, and therefore assumes a different tone. He is absolutely without zeal or the spirit of proselytism. He has nothing to say of the beneficent influence of sweetness and light; he seems rather disposed to think that when the whole truth is known existence may become unbearable; that the planets in which life is extinct are probably those in which criticism has achieved its work. He eschews controversy, and takes little interest in the questions which occupy the thoughts of men. His aims are purely speculative, and have no relevancy to contemporaneous events. He is an artist, seated on the brow of a hill, who sketches the landscape, but has nothing in common with the herds that graze upon the plain below. He is in fact a quietist, and from the eminence of his exceptional position surveys the world with a feeling akin to that which a spirit from some higher sphere might be supposed to have in contemplating the busy, fussy little ants that jostle one another on this mole-hill of an earth. God is only an idea; nature exists, but is unmoral; good and evil are alike indifferent to her; and history, from an ethical point of view, is a permanent scandal. This is the final word of culture as revealed by Renan, and he naturally enough partakes of the Buddhist temper, to which annihilation appears to be the supreme good. And this is doubtless the mood which culture, as understood by the critical school, tends to produce. Its intellectual principle is pantheism, its ethical principle is the identity of the good and the beautiful, and historically it evolves itself either into the animalism of the senses or into the quietism of a fatalistic philosophy; and whichever form it assumes, it must inevitably fail to make reason and the will of God prevail.

But one may surely be a lover of culture without being forced to adopt the principles of Renan and Arnold, — as one may be reasonable and yet hold to positive beliefs; as one may have taste without denying conscience.

Culture may indeed easily become the insidious foe of revealed religion, but it may also be its serviceable ally; and since in our day many of the most thoroughly trained and versatile minds are employed in the service of unbelief, it is certainly most desirable, and from a human point of view even necessary, that they be met by intellects of equal discipline and power. We are living in an epoch of transition. The decay of faith in the Protestant sects is accelerated by the consciousness that their existence is a contradiction of the fundamental principle of Protestantism; and among Catholics a wide-spread indifference, and new modes of thought created by the scientific developments of the age, have cooled the zeal and weakened the faith of many. The wavering of religious belief has unsettled all other things, so that nothing seems any longer to rest upon a firm and immovable basis. The new theories are in the air, and precautionary measures are ineffectual, at least with regard to society in general. There has never been a time in the world's history, in which the influence of literature was so all-pervading as at present, and this power is in great measure anonymous and irresponsible. Reviews and newspapers discuss everything and are read by everybody, so that any youth is prepared to pronounce you an authoritative judgment as to whether there is a God. The gravest and most sacred subjects are treated in a mock-serious tone which is worse than open blasphemy. The old Protestant controversy is as obsolete as the dress of the Pilgrim Fathers. Questions of grace, election, and free-will, have ceased to have any interest for men who, insisting upon their right of private judgment and the supremacy of the individual mind, are puzzled to know whether God and the soul exist; and the famous ministerial jousts, in which the doughty champions were wont to brandish their favorite texts like flaming swords, have lost their dramatic effect and are grown altogether tame in the eyes of a generation which hears every day that the Bible itself is but the fairy tale of an ignorant and superstitious age. The old disputes will doubtless survive for a time, and individuals and even classes may be helped by them, but the real issue, so far as the active mind of the age is concerned, has already been transferred to quite other grounds, and it is our immediate and urgent duty to fit ourselves for the new conflict, which is not between the Church and the sects, but between the Church and infidelity. The argument is to be made fundamental and exhaustive. All philosophies and sciences are to be interrogated; all literatures to be studied; all forms of belief are to be analyzed; all methods are to be used; and the infinitely great and the infinitesimally small are to be required to give up their secret. The religious import of the sciences is precisely what lends to this study its mysterious charm. The physical comfort which may be derived from a wider and truer acquaintance with nature is of minor importance. That which the philosopher and the man of the world are yearning to learn from all this eager and ceaseless peering into the forms and workings of matter is whether or not any authentic response will be given to the eternal questionings of the human heart about God, the soul, and the life that is to be. This restlessness and scepticism is doubtless pathological. If men had faith, they would not be tormented by the feverish anxiety to surprise God in the mysteries which he has hidden from human eye; but they have no faith, and since it is impossible for the mind to remain indifferent to the infinite mystery which is everywhere in all that it sees and thinks, therefore do men who have ceased to believe seek to satisfy by knowledge the inborn craving of the soul for some tidings from the inner truth of things. They will take nothing for granted, but make God himself questionable. And here at once we may perceive the arduousness of the task which is imposed upon those who are called to the defence of the faith in our day. The first step their adversaries take leads into the bottomless abyss of endless speculation and doubt. In the Protestant controversy there was the common and certain ground of the Written Word, to which in the confusion of debate it was possible to return to take bearings, while the deists of the last century agreed with their opponents in admitting the existence of God as indisputably evident to the natural reason. But the new phase of infidelity would make knowledge itself inconclusive in all matters where our concern is with the absolute truth of things. It denies that there is any such truth, or at least that it is discoverable by man. I find in all the current theories of unbelief the assumption that all that can be known is the relative, and that the highest conceivable philosophy is only phenomenology. With men who hold such opinions it is impossible to reason from fixed principles. The old methods fail to reach them. All the syllogisms that can be strung together can never compass a higher truth than that which is given in the original intuition, and if this does not attain to the reality underlying the phenomenon neither will our conclusions. The assumption that knowledge is only the perception of relations makes all discussions as to what anything is in itself appear futile and childish. Hence the contempt of the modern schools for metaphysics and the scholastic methods. The great practical difficulty, as I take it, in successfully controverting the new theories lies in the fact that they represent modes of viewing things rather than states of mind. They are not held as conclusions from unanswerable arguments, but as a way of accounting for phenomena which is justified by the convergence of innumerable plausibilities toward a given line of thought. It is considered to be enough that they are in accord with the tendencies of the age, and in harmony with the great time-spirit, who, as these philosophers teach, has usurped the throne of the Eternal and Omnipotent God. A few words will suffice to sketch in general outline this system, and at the same time to show how widely it prevails. It is assumed that God is not or cannot be known to be, and as philosophy is phenomenology, it starts with matter in the state in which it is possible for the mind first to detect it. Space is filled with incandescent gas, star-dust, from which the sidereal systems are evolved. This view, for the correctness of which many arguments are adduced, receives additional weight from the study of our own planet, which, beginning as an incandescent mass, has during long ages been gradually cooling. When life first appears it is in its lowest forms, and there is progression up to man. To this point it is maintained the astronomer and the geologist are able to conduct us. The zoologist now comes to trace the descent of man, as the geologist has followed the evolution of the globe, and Darwin and others find that he has been developed by natural processes from the lowest forms of life. The question of man's special endowments thus presents itself, and the psychologist attempts to show that thought is transformed sensation, and will, transformed emotion, as man is a transformed animal.

The principle of evolution is applied to the history of language and of races in philology and ethnology, and these sciences are made auxiliary to the new theories. The sociologist next appears, to unravel the infinitely complicated and intricate network of human relations, and to point out how this marvellous and entangled scheme is but the product of a few rudimentary instincts. And finally, the philosopher of history proposes to account for the whole life and all the achievements of the human race by the aid of fatalistic laws. Given the race, and its surroundings, and he will offer you a mechanical rule by which you will be able to explain everything, — religion, literature, and social institutions. It would, of course, be beside my present purpose to stop to point out the absurdities and the gaps in all this, but what I wish to call attention to is the fact that this is a way of looking at the universe, and that little or nothing is gained by insisting upon errors in detail or by showing that certain data of science are in accord with revealed truth. The fault is radical and universal, and the only effective method of dealing with it is to be sought in a comprehensive philosophy, which, starting from a true theory of knowledge will embrace the whole range of science, and by correcting the false interpretations of its data, will educate men and lead them to see that a theory of the universe which excludes God is not only unintelligible, but destructive of the essential principles of reason. The intellectual difficulties with which the present generation of believers have to contend are greater than in any past age. It is not possible to laugh at our adversaries unless we are content to make ourselves ridiculous. In matters of this kind sarcasm and vituperation are not only out of place, but are no better than the language of the devil. Smart hits intended for the crowd fail of effect even with the masses.

That in the end, and after never so much science and theory, the perfect wisdom of humble and trusting faith will be made only the more evident is in no way doubtful; but in the meantime we may not stand as idle lookers-on, and as though we had no part or concern in this mighty and painful conflict.

It was a principle with St. Ignatius of Loyola that a Christian should have the faith which hopes everything from God, and then act as though he expected nothing except from his own exertions.

No maxim could be more applicable to the emergency of which I am writing. I know that our blessed Lord is with his Church, and that he can turn our ignorance and supineness to the good of those who love him. I know that whatever we may do we are useless servants. The prayer of the humble is better than the thoughts of the learned, and a great saint is able to do a holier work than the most perfectly cultivated genius.

All this is indisputable, and one benefit to be hoped for from a higher culture would be the power to realize more truly what we are so ready to admit in theory. My words, if addressed to those devout and saintly souls who with unutterable groanings raise to God the voice of prayer which penetrates the heavens, would be an impertinence. It may well be that were it not for these just ones we should all perish. My thought is lower and is intended for those who, in the midst of a thousand imperfections, feel that they are better fitted to fight in the plain below than to lift up hands of supplication on the holy mount.

The issue indeed is in God's keeping, but we must strive to quit ourselves like men, and as though all depended upon our skill and courage. Without thorough training and mental discipline we shall only cumber the ground and block the way.

# CHAPTER VII.

### PATRIOTISM.

> AND Thou, O God, of whom we hold
> Our country and our Freedom fair,
> Within Thy tender love enfold
> This land; for all Thy people care.
> Uplift our hearts above our fortunes high,
> Let not the good we have make us forget
> The better things that in Thy heavens lie !
> Keep, still, amid the fever and the fret
> Of all this eager life, our thoughts on Thee,
> The Hope, the Strength, the God of all the Free.

LOVE of country springs from so many sources which have their fountain-head in our inmost being that it scarcely needs commending; and it has found such abundant and varied expression in the art and literature of all nations that it is difficult to praise it without falling into commonplace. Each one seems to himself, if he go not beyond primitive, unreflecting consciousness, a separate, independent being, whose thought, love, and deeds are determined simply by his own personality. A little attention, however, will show him that whatever he sees, knows, and feels is part of himself. As his body is kept living by the constant assimilation of food and air, so his mind and heart are kept alive and active through communion with what may be perceived and understood, or admired and loved. The ties which bind us to earth and heaven, to air and water, the sympathies which unite us with whatever is beautiful, true, or good, the attractions which draw us to beings like and yet unlike ourselves, are but forms of self-love. We find and love in what is not ourselves that which we need to round and complete our lives. The desire to grow toward and into all things is the divine spark in our nature, the impulse which makes us yearn for more knowledge, more love, more happiness, more possessions. We tend ultimately to identify ourselves with God and His universe and the objects and persons we learn to know and love are the stepping-stones in the ascent toward the divine life. The instinct for local and personal attachments is born in us; it is found in the mere animal, — the horse knows his stall, the dog loves his master. Our fondness for things and persons is not wholly determined by their qualities. The cottage of the poor is cherished more than the palace of the rich; the most helpless child is often a mother's darling. Bleak and cheerless Lapland is loved as truly as Italy, dowered with beauty's fatal gift. The spot where our young years were passed, as in a dream, the persons by whom we were then surrounded, seem fair and good to us. The memory of them is intertwined with all our thoughts; they are part of ourselves. The very sorrows we knew with them are sweeter than the joys we now can taste. Our souls never lose the tinge of the colors with which they were then imbued. We bear with us into distant lands, through long years, the memories of that dewy dawn, of that fresh springtime when all things seemed created anew and a smile of God rested upon His world. With the love of home and of those who made it home, the love of country first begins to stir within the heart; for our country is and remains our fatherland, the land where we knew a father's and a mother's love. This is the meaning of the Greek word "patriotism;" it is the love of the fathers; of their thoughts and hopes; of their deeds and aspirations. It is therefore something far higher and deeper than a mere attachment to places, though fair and pleasant they be. Our sympathy with nature, however, is very real. We feel a kinship with stars and flowers; we are uplifted by mountains; we are awed by the ocean; we are fresh and happy with spring; we are sober and subdued with autumn; and this general feeling becomes tenderer and more human when it is associated with what is dear to us for reasons personal to ourselves. In this way the scenery in which our home is set, by which our country is characterized, touches us more nearly, awakens more grateful and delightful thoughts than aught we can behold elsewhere. If we are moulded by our surroundings we also help to create them, and objects which for years we have been accustomed to look upon day by day have for us a meaning and a sacredness, a charm and a beauty which they lose when viewed by the indifferent eyes of strangers. Thus the physical features of the fatherland, whether noble or common, impress the imagination and color the souls of the children; they enter into our patriotic feelings, as the face, the voice, the gestures of one we love seem to become part of our love. When the German remembers the Rhine, with its vine-clad hills and feudal castles, his heart thrills with emotion for the whole German land. The Irishman who turns to Erin feels his pulse beat quicker when he thinks of the glories of Wicklow and Killarney. And so all men are pleased with the natural excellences and beauties of their country; the fertility of its soil, the salubrity and temperateness of its climate, its high mountains, its deep valleys, its mighty rivers, its bays and inlets, its islands and solemn woods, its waterfalls, casting their white incense to heaven, — all help to make it precious and dear; and it becomes still dearer when genius or heroism has thrown its light upon nature's charms. Monuments like the Cathedral of Cologne, or Westminster Abbey, or St. Peter's in Rome, are centres of patriotic feeling. The emigrant to far lands thinks of them with a sentiment akin to that of the Israelite in captivity: "By the waters of Babylon we sat down and wept, when we remembered thee, O Sion!" "If I forget thee, O Jerusalem! let my right hand forget her cunning." The ruins of what our forefathers built, the battlefields whereon they shed their blood for right and freedom, the graves where their bones are buried make sacred the land. But these local attachments and associations, sweet and holy though they are, and inseparable from right feeling are not of the essence of patriotism; for our true human world is spiritual, not material; the city of the soul, and not that in which the body tabernacles, is our country.

When in some foreign land we hear the sacred name spoken, in the old familiar mother-tongue, and our pulse quickens, and our eye brightens, and our bosom heaves, and the speaker — whom perchance we have never seen before — seems to be our brother, our emotion is caused by something higher and purer than local attachments and memories. We live in the spirit or not at all; and the material things we possess or strive for seem good to us because we believe they are serviceable to the higher life of thought and love. A sentiment in common, a deep, far pervading feeling that animates a collective body as with one soul, is what makes a national consciousness. Fertile fields may be made waste, cities desolate, rivers dry; the ruins of the homes of our youth may be trodden by the hoofs of beasts, friends may turn from us, and civil strife rend the land, but the love of country still burns with its steady, inextinguishable glow within our hearts. We love the fatherland, not alone or chiefly for the food it gives, the property it protects, the security it provides; we love it above all for the richer, freer, nobler human life which it makes possible: not so much for its high mountains, its wide-spreading plains, its broad rivers, its thundering cataracts, its pleasant and bracing air, as for the noble freedom, the generous love, the great thoughts which enter into and determine the national spirit and character. Our country is the symbol of all that is most priceless on earth, — liberty, truth, devotion, loyalty. Its name is intertwined with the memories, hopes, loves, and aspirations of all our life; it is as dear to us as that of our mother, as full of sweet suggestiveness as that of home, as near to our hearts as the names of the friends we most love. At its invocation our whole nature changes: if timid, we become brave; if hard, sympathetic; if selfish, generous. We turn from wealth and pleasant company and the most cherished pursuits if that sacred name ring out in the bugle call, and, throwing all things away, we rush forward to defy danger and death that we may save our country's honor and independence. "It is a pleasant and a glorious thing," says Horace, " to die for one's country;" and no line of ancient poetry has evoked a more universal response. Whatever else may change or wholly pass away, patriotism is as imperishable as religion, as immortal as love; for to all wellborn hearts the native land is forever dear, whether strong and free or helpless and in chains. The memory of its glories and triumphs descends through a hundred generations, and when the people itself perishes, the deeds of its heroes become the property of the whole race of man. Through a thousand years of suffering and sorrow, of tyranny and oppression, the heavenly passion still lives, and from out the gloom, the lovers of their country look to God, waiting in hope, till the dawn of a better day shall break, bringing promise of freedom and new life.

What land, what people, has the sun ever illumined more worthy of the heart's deep affection than our own? Here, where Nature, who never hastens and never tires, has stored, through countless ages, whatever may be serviceable to man, divine Providence has given us a country as large as all Europe, with a soil more fertile, and a climate more invigorating. We have come into possession of it, not as ignorant and lawless barbarians, but as civilized men, with conscious purposes, with high ideals, the inheritors of all the knowledge and wisdom of the past, and having in our hands whatever implements and weapons human skill has invented to strengthen and enlarge the power of man. Across the great ocean our ancestors bore the blessings of Christian civilization, leaving behind them the narrowness and hatreds, the political and social wrongs with which it had become associated. Never did a continent pass under the control of a new race with so little injustice, so little violence and cruelty; never were states founded by men more true-hearted, honest, and brave; never were great and memorable triumphs gained by fairer means; never was a commonwealth made to rest on broader or more humane principles.

It is the planting of the American colonies which makes the discovery of Columbus the opening of a new era in the history of mankind. Here the Christian people saw the light dawn toward which through a thousand years of darkness and struggle they had been groping. Here God's infinite goodness revealed itself, offering opportunities for freer and nobler life to all alike, without distinction of race or creed or sex, even as upon all His sun shines and His rain falls. The patriots who made the Declaration of Independence, the statesmen and warriors who led the people through the long and doubtful struggle of the Revolution, felt that they were building better than they knew. Never were heroes more conscious that the cause they battled for was God's and all men's. In their words, and in their deeds there breathes a lofty and unselfish spirit, which, to the end of time, shall thrill every true and generous heart. Their work has prospered beyond the utmost vision of seers, beyond the fondest dreams of poets. The little republic they founded has grown, in a century, to be the strongest, the most progressive, the most enlightened, and the most firmly established civil power in the world. In virtue of its constitutional vitality and assimilative force, it has spread from the Atlantic to the Pacific, from the Canadian border to the everglades of Florida. Decade after decade it has sent farther and farther west colonists who, as by a kind of instinct, became the founders of prosperous states. The great Civil War, which threatened to disrupt it, but purified its constitution and opened to it a larger and less impeded career. In the old world whoever is straitened or oppressed, whoever yearns for richer life and wider opportunities, turns with longing to America. However much we may lack, as individuals, the culture and breeding, the repose and dignity of manner which distinguish the true gentleman or the perfect lady, as a people we are the most attractive; and the charm of our national life lies not so much in our freedom, or in anything we have already accomplished, as in the promise it gives of nobler things. Here the largest thought and the widest love which have ever been brought to bear upon the polities of men are at work to mould the coming race. Here is liberty; here is good will; here is willingness; here is invitation to all; here is opportunity, beckoning to every faculty of the human soul. "Never," says Emerson, "never country had such a fortune, as men call fortune, as this, in its geography, its history, and in its majestic possibilities." But let not our patriotism run to foolish vanity; let us not imagine because our country is great we also are great; let us rather dread lest in a noble land we ourselves be found ignorant and vulgar. The wise are never boastful, and they who best understand the priceless worth of America feel how far above them is the ideal of public and private virtue of which America is the symbol. He is the truest patriot who strives day by day to make himself worthy of such a country, turning away from no labor, no hardship, no self-denial, which may help him to become an honest, honorable, enlightened, and religious man. Who is there among us who would not be willing to die for his country? Let us learn that to live for it is a yet higher and more useful thing; that the task it sets each one of us is not in any way beneath a hero's courage, a philosopher's insight, or a poet's love. Weath and numbers we have, and all the strength which material civilization can give. What we lack is a new man to represent fitly this new world. Great things must be balanced by great characters, or matter will prevail over spirit, and the soul become inferior to its setting. "It is certain," says Emerson again, "that our civilization is yet incomplete; it has not ended nor given sign of ending in a hero. It is a wild democracy,— the riot of mediocrities, dishonesties, and fudges."

The special vice of the American is the breathless haste with which he works for success, which he generally takes to mean money. Whatever is restful, as reflection and meditation, gives him qualms of conscience; he is ashamed to be at leisure. He thinks, watch in hand, as he eats, with his eye on the daily market-report. He seems always afraid lest he forget or neglect something, and so miss an opportunity to gain a dollar. This workingman's haste, this alertness for a chance to turn a penny, is fatal to distinction of thought and behavior; it destroys the sense for form, for proportion, and grace. Hence this type of American, in all the relations of life, is quick, sharp, and abrupt. In his intercourse with friends and relations, with women and children, he is preoccupied by thoughts of business, and seems to say: "Appreciate my politeness, for time is money." His natural inclination is to marry a wife with as little ceremony as he buys a horse. Joyful occasions are almost as unwelcome to him as the sad, for both alike are interruptions of business. If he is poor he works with the hope of becoming rich; if he is rich he works from dread of poverty. He cannot take recreation without apology, as though he should say, "I beg pardon, but my health or my wife's requires this of me." He writes a letter in the style of a telegram, and would prefer to talk only through a telephone from fear of being buttonholed. He looks forward to the time when he shall travel a hundred instead of fifty miles an hour; and in his rapid journeys he is all the while thinking or talking of business or politics, which for him is mainly a question of finance. The men in whom he takes interest are money men and politicians. In his spare moments he reads the newspapers, which are filled with whatever concerns trade and material progress, interspersed with accounts of all kinds of crime. His idea of pleasure is sport. He admires a horse more for the price it brings than for beauty and grace; a pugilist more for the money than the victory he wins. He measures all things by the same standard. A book, a preacher, a play, like a mine or a railway, are worth what they will sell for in the market. What is dear is fine, and he will even submit to all sorts of discomfort if it is expensive. A poet is an idle, foolish being, for poetry, unless some freak of fashion give it value, is unsalable. Dancing is a good enough pursuit, if one knows how to make it lucrative. He easily breaks forth into abuse of the very rich, for it is natural to abuse one's more successful rivals.

The gospel of work and utility has been preached to us and imposed on us, until we all have become or are in danger of becoming the drudges and victims of the uneasy and insatiable demon of greed. The ideal is the possession of more and more, and in striving for this we forget and lose ourselves,— lose even the power to enjoy the wealth for which we sacrificed all that makes life good and pleasant. To add to the trouble, we seem no longer to be free. We lack self-control, and are borne onward by this material movement, as the crest is carried by the wave. We have lost relish for a life which is simple, pure, moderate, and healthful. We are the victims of an environment, and to survive at all, we feel we must survive as money-getters. That the majority now believe in this Mammon-worship is no proof that it is not a degrading and idolatrous worship. "The majority are bad," said one of the wise men of Greece; we at least may say that they are unthinking and heedless of the best. They need the guidance and the strength which are found in the wisdom and example of the few; but we hitch our most gifted men to the drays of commerce and the machinery of manufacture, where they are goaded on, and driven to death by the tyranny of competition. They should be treated like coursers, which for the most part are idle, nursing the strength that renders them capable of memorable deeds. We boast of our industrial captains, who stand at the head of great material enterprises, not perceiving that their work, like that of the unhappy beings they employ, prevents them from becoming men; for, however many millions of money they may have, they have low thoughts and feeble faith and love. If we love our country, let us not be afraid to speak even unpleasant truth in this age when it has grown to be the fashion to lie to the people, as formerly men lied to kings.

There is no better measure of the progress of an individual than the degree of his ability to stand alone, in thought and action, undisturbed by the adverse opinions and judgments of his fellow-men. He who leads his own life is a real, not an artificial, man. Let us believe in the worth of character, and while we strive to upbuild our own, let us also seek to spread this faith, which is fundamental for all who would uphold popular government. When the people are a herd they are easily swayed and ruled by one man; when they are individualized, the dominion of one is not possible. Let us hold and teach that better than millions of money or cattle, is a brave heart, a hopeful temper, an enlightened mind, a cheerful and appreciative soul, content in quiet virtue, and able to take delight in familiar things and in the common blessings which God sends to all.

Let us dread whatever is hard or exaggerated or vulgar; whatever shows lack of delicacy of thought or purity of conduct; whatever springs from a spirit of false audacity or foolish boastfulness. Let our patriotism be a sort of religion, urging us to elevation, seriousness, and chastity of thought and desire; for, after all, our confidence that popular government is the best rests on faith, not on knowledge. Let us make ourselves wise and helpful, strong and self-contained, whether we are happy or unhappy. What gives pleasure is of little moment; what gives power and wisdom is all-important. Let us make true Emerson's prophecy: "Trade and government will not alone be the favored aims, but every useful, every elegant art, every exercise of imagination, the height of reason, the noblest affection, the purest religion will find their home in our institutions, and write our laws for the benefit of men."

THE END.